A journey through time with Louise which will give you an insight into a positive mind and what a line of questioning can really help you to achieve.

As a motivational leader, NLP therapist and life coach, Louise explains her thought processes throughout her tales of tragedy and loss. On a mission to help others succeed and live their dreams while she takes her own journey to the next level, she simplifies the message of positivity.

I would like to dedicate this book to my beautiful family
and friends (those who are on this planet and those who
have been delivered elsewhere) who have always been so
supportive of everything I do—giving me the confidence
and love to march forward on this amazing journey.

Thank you

Contents

Who is that person I read about

Here I am again, sat in a popular coffee shop on a quite dismal day, sipping away at my grande vanilla latte as various characters bustle through the main walkway. Yes I'm here and doing it: writing to you. One of the promises I made to myself a couple of years ago (Lou, you must find time to do what you really want to do in life).

Having had so many people question me over the years 'how did you get through that' and 'how did you cope with that', I thought I would have a complete change of direction one day and try to help others understand the power of their own thoughts. At that time of my life, I hadn't stumbled across NLP (neuro linguistic programming) but I did know that I managed in a way that some others couldn't comprehend.

After years of listening to motivational speakers and reading books in order to become someone who could also help others, I realised that it wasn't all as helpful as I had first believed. Although so many people are touched by motivational speakers and follow them through social media, there is still quite a lot of bad press surrounding some of the high profile speakers. The number of people who found such speakers and gurus unhelpful surprised me. I've read how they are out of touch with reality and how easy they make turning your life around seem, with very little understanding of how tough it can be when you are not 'them'.

Although I come across so many inspirational quotes and positive stories on social media, I have equally found some extremely controversial outlooks on how positive all of this actually leaves you feeling. Have you ever seen in your newsfeed, stream or feed, posts after posts about how you should be feeling or looking at life? Are there constant messages of how amazing everyone else is feeling and how wonderful their lives are? Do you ever feel like deleting the very positive messages that you subscribed to or chose to follow?

Sometimes I feel that all the published positivity is just one big PR and marketing trip for the leader to make a living out of people who are trying their best to get through a rocky journey. I don't have any issue with people putting their good skills to use and making a living out of it, certainly not, but I do have an issue with not giving the time to people to explain fully the steps required to be in that 'zone'. A single quote isn't going to change your entire approach unless you really know what it means and believe in it—or better still, believe in you.

I personally feel that many of these great speakers and writers are very helpful and have a great morale edge when delivering their stories but that's because I don't just listen to the stories and feel uplifted, I actually understand the process. How can you truly relate to the process and move forward in your life if you don't understand it?

To simply see the results of someone who has come from a bad beginning or maybe suffered a little—sometimes even a lot—isn't always enough to help you understand how to apply their techniques to your own life. None of it truly helps when you go back to your day-to-day life and are faced with your own battles and fears, unless you fully understand the process.

Throughout my book I am going to give you insight into my thought processes through the hard times I have faced. I want to let you into the secrets of positivity by using examples from my own extensive experiences—you can even use this book as a manual or work-book which you can later refer back to. There is room for you to try some great exercises and techniques.

You see, no positive person in the limelight wants you to know the real truth—the reality of what being positive actually means, because as if you had a true insight into their thoughts and beliefs, you may not think as highly of them, and worse still, you may not pay them.

We are told to surround ourselves with positive people, but do we all know what that actually means, and the effects of doing so?

Let me start by explaining that I am regarded as a very positive person, I have been called inspirational countless times and many people have come to me seeking advice, questioning my thought processes and even my resilience. These are everyday people from all walks of life; some are my peers, colleagues and family members, others are complete strangers who have contacted me after press releases and radio interviews.

Delivering motivational talks is something that I enjoy very much and often the people who question me have been inspired by a talk. There is no particular 'type' of person that has felt touched by the messages I deliver, some have been through tragic circumstances in life and others have not, regardless, the message is usually taken in the same way. How do I know that my message is taken in this positive way? I know because I have been told verbally and in writing, I can feel it when I deliver my talks and meet new people, and I can feel it when giving advice to the people who ask for it.

When I look at my audience and see the eye contact and body language, I know they're relating. It's not just the things that are said, it's the un-spoken too. By using your five magical senses you can pick up a lot.

We all gather information which is instrumental in forming an opinion or belief about ourselves and others. We have been doing this since the day we were born—a huge amount of information that has been gathered by someone in their mid-thirties. How we then use this information is what determines how we develop throughout our lives and how much self-belief we have. This is why I am so interested in speaking with as many people as possible in order to gather as much information as possible. The fact is, not only does it help them, but in turn, it helps me.

This information helps me drive forward to become more successful, and it gives me a much greater understanding of myself, and of others around me.

Perhaps it is hardly a wonder that some people do not feel inspired by the story outcome of the motivational leader on stage, if that leader has arrived in a helicopter. However touching his or her story of poverty or tragedy was, the audience just couldn't relate to the slick, current image before them. Or maybe sometimes it is a simple lack of self-belief within the audience members. Either way, a gap exists that separates the motivator from the audience.

Some of the people I have spoken to after a talk were left feeling completely energised, motivated and determined. They felt that they could go on to do those things they want to do. They felt energised throughout the talk and even perhaps for an hour after, but then what happened to the majority? They were back in their reality with only one story more to tell. The belief that other people are so much more positive and capable than them had a detrimental effect.

Sometimes seeing these leaders on stage, watching them on TV or reading their books, can leave people feeling like there is something wrong with them for not feeling positive 100% of the time. Clearly these leaders must be positive people all the time right? To be where they are now and to do what they do, preaching to others, means that they have it all figured out right?

The moment you are left with these negative thoughts, the issue of feeling even more distant from the person you would like to become arises; your self-belief can be drastically reduced.

This is why it is important to understand the truth behind the people that you see on stage or in the books you read. It's not as simple as overcoming every hurdle or becoming a positive person all the time—they make it look so easy!

Feeling that separation from the person on the stage before-you is entirely down to your own thoughts, and not due to the person in front of you. In all my studying and experience with coaching and therapy, it is more apparent than ever before that you are the one with the control of your success. Do you think the motivational speakers in front of you believe in themselves and push through all negativity, realising that there is no limit to how far they can go?

The biggest reason for me to write this book is the need to tell you the process, to explain the thought processes that are most destructive to us, and to shed some light on the positive people that surround you, in order to help you relate to them. If you already relate to them and have no problems with negative thoughts, then lucky you—you are a master of thoughts and are perhaps one of those people that others aspire to be like but may sometimes not understand. The more people understand the more people can be helped.

I've been working with a number of clients who have never delved into their thought processes before and have spent many years on a negative journey wondering why they feel so incapable. Once we have consciously picked the thoughts apart, and more importantly, looked at the reality of their thoughts along with a better alternative thought process which provides options to look at things in a number of different ways, it becomes clear that the client starts to feel empowered and free. The realisation that you have this control can open up so many doors and take away all those limits you place on yourself. You'll see more of how this works when I reveal my thoughts during the rock bottom times in my life. I will tell you the stories, but along with those stories, I will share my mind.

Self-belief and where it comes from

So what is it all about? What does any of that actually mean?

In simple terms, your belief system has dictated who and what you have become, throughout your life. Thankfully, though, your belief system has a fantastic quality—it is changeable. This means that if you have believed something to be a concrete, immovable truth, such as a judgement about your basic nature, you might just find that you can move to another version of truth via a little thought and awareness. If you are willing to change how you see things and to grow, you soon realise that you can be or do whatever you want and you are not actually stuck as 'who you are' at all.

Imagine, if you can alter your thoughts and see things from a completely different angle, implement a shift in the way you do things and mould yourself into something new, you become an entirely different person. Your story doesn't change, but you do. You may believe that people view you in the same way as they always have, and when that feeling or thought process is in place, that too can affect your self-belief system, making it easier to remain in your comfort zone where people recognise you.

It's important to get a good understanding of this as it helps us to become aware of the reasons why people are so different and how we can make as many changes to our personality, thought processes and even circumstances as we want.

You may come across as a natural optimist or pessimist but many scientists, therapists and psychologists believe that this is not actually the case, that it is more to do with your internal mapping (the journey you have been on and the information you have taken in over the years). Optimism isn't just about a few positive affirmations and feeling happy, it's a learned behaviour which is developed over time. So much of what we do is habit and that is true also of our self-belief system (the way we think of ourselves).

Studies show that only 20% of our optimism is genetic and the rest is acquired by learning throughout our lives; the same goes for pessimism. Making a committed decision to become a more optimistic person is the first step towards changing your perspective, but it's not as simple as just that; you need to apply the process that's discussed through this book and work on your thought processes until positive beliefs come naturally to you.

The information you take in has huge consequences for your self-belief system, especially if it is coming from experts—the experts being your parents in most cases. According to NLP, when we are young, we take in every word that is said about us and to us; this forms our opinion of ourselves before we have had time to make an opinion of our own based on our own experience in life.

Our teachers, friends, parents of our friends, grandparents and then later on in life, our colleagues and employers, all have a huge part to play in our self-belief system. Throughout the years we are indoctrinated and a solid opinion of how we are perceived is formed. We then mould ourselves to this perception, whether it is positive or negative.

The child that is told they can never do something because they haven't got a talent for it will take in and store this information. Only when they have tried and failed or tried and succeeded will the proof be there for them, but very seldom is that real proof, it's based on what they already believed before even trying. The child that is told they are not good enough at something is more likely to give up after failing at it once than the child who has been told they have a natural talent.

Another example is the time I was told how awful a neighbourhood was, apparently it was full of drug addicts and low income areas with no potential for anyone who was looking for a job. I was told that businesses were always closing and it was a deprived area. When visiting this area with the knowledge I already had, it was very difficult to see the beautiful architecture and business people having lunch over wine; instead I was drawn more towards the boarded up shop on the corner and the small gang of people hanging out smoking and swearing. An opinion of this place had been formed from one brief visit and I then told others about it. Visiting it again at a different time in my life, I noticed everything except what I had seen previously.

I could see the beautiful architecture and Tudor buildings that held sweet boutique shops with their owners working hard to keep their customers happy and stay in business. I could see the business people laughing over lunch and working on their laptops, enjoying their surroundings. It's sad to think that I was able to form an opinion of such a place based on another person's idea. I have no doubt that the areas they spoke of exist but like most locations and most situations in life, there are two sides, it just depends on what side you want to see.

The person who has been told throughout their life that they will manage and pull through, has much more chance of actually doing just that than someone who is used to receiving less positive statements. To be told something like that is more than just encouraging; it feeds our self-belief system and empowers us. To be told this throughout our lives by numerous people or to believe that this is what others think we are capable of can actually give us the belief that we genuinely have the capability to do just that.

How we view the world

We all look at the world in slightly different ways and that is all down to this perception and internal mapping of ours. Your experiences arm you with knowledge and sometimes it can be very difficult to change an opinion on something when you feel you **know** how it really is. *Your* reality however, varies from other people's reality and this is why you should never second guess what someone is thinking or feeling, no matter how well you think you know them; their belief system will be different. There are too many communication issues between people in life and this is often down to the number of misinterpretations. When you second guess what a person is feeling or what they mean, you are instantly relating their situation to one of your own; you will be comparing the emotions you have experienced and think that you fully understand them based on how you have felt.

You may also take into consideration the other person's history (if you know them well enough) but again, there are gaps. Unless you have the same thought processes, intensity of emotions, the same fears, self-belief system and so on, it's virtually impossible to fully understand.

You can empathise based on your own experiences and get a close understanding when all the details are articulated, which is usually welcomed when someone is confiding in you, but it's always a good idea to remain open with this understanding.

Too many people in conversation now do not listen properly; instead they are comparing your story to their own while you are talking and even thinking of what they want to say to you next. When you truly listen to someone and take in what they're saying, you hear so much more, and rather than second guess, why not try asking what they mean exactly, or how they feel exactly, just as a coach or therapist would? If you want to invest your time in people and have a greater understanding of them as individuals, this is always something to bear in mind. This approach helps with so many communication issues within friend and family circles, in the workplace and even in your relationship, it encourages you to grow together.

I was given an exercise to do on a coaching weekend quite some time ago and it still makes me think when I am explaining myself to others even now.

In this exercise, a large group of us was given a task to complete; we were each handed a shoelace that had been tied together in many places, forming a loop. Our task was to undo the loop without making the shoelace any longer. We were given a list of spoken instructions and one of the trainers told us a story about how someone cheeky in their last group used a small pen knife from her hand-bag to cut the shoelace, he then proceeded to laugh and say 'please do not do this'. On the desk in front of us were straws and scissors but no one decided to cut the shoelace before our time was up. Having all failed the task miserably, we were asked how we could have completed it; someone called out saying it was impossible as we weren't allowed to cut the shoelace. The trainer asked where we had heard the instructions that we were not allowed to cut the shoelace. Ah, we had all presumed we were not allowed to cut the shoelace but the actual instructions didn't state that we were not allowed to use the scissors. We had all presumed this was the case due to the way the trainer had explained what the lady had done in his previous group; we had drawn on our previous experiences in life to make a decision on what was wrong or right and filled in the gaps that were missing ourselves.

The number of existing knots in the shoelaces we were given was due to the amount of times the loops had been cut from previous groups. They understood the instructions differently and therefore had cut the loops with the scissors.

The gap in misinterpretation comes when people have different intent behind what they say, compared to your understanding of it. For example, "you never wash the dishes" may actually mean, "I wash the dishes a lot more than you do and you don't seem to wash them up over the weekends." With so many gaps in our communication, we tend to fill the gaps in ourselves with our own beliefs which can lead to communication break-downs. Obviously we all have to use our common sense as well but rather than second guess most of the time and take a lazy approach to communication, or a higher ground when communicating, (by thinking we know best) we would all be much better off and live with more peace if we took the trouble to find out a little more.

I was speaking to someone only last week who was explaining to me why he would never buy a house and how important it was to rent and save the rest of their money.

I disagreed with this instantly (not out loud but my mind went into over-drive). He was convinced and **knew** that it was a risky decision that often goes wrong; to do *the right* thing by him, he wouldn't put so much money down as a deposit on a house. My opinion on this matter was the complete opposite and in my earlier days, I would have stood my ground and explained how buying a property was *the right* thing to do and how his theory was *wrong*. Instead, I asked questions; I wanted to know why and where his theory came from. It transpires that after witnessing his parents go bankrupt and being told for years about all the risks and the reason why his parents have decided to stay in rented accommodation, a strong opinion had been formed: it was now a fact to them.

This person's reality is different from mine but that doesn't mean that there is a right or wrong; it is the right choice for them only if it fits with their beliefs and their values. My job in this conversation was then to see if he was open to any alternative beliefs. If he has made a decision that he feels comfortable with and that he sees the benefit of, then that decision works for him, but to listen to other people *telling* him that this is the wrong decision makes me want to scream out the *real* facts, which are:

If such a decision fits well with your priorities, your environment and your belief, then it **could** be the right decision for you—at least for now.

- If you are nervous about the security of your job and you think that there is a possibility that you would struggle to keep up your mortgage payments, then it **could** be the right decision for you—at least for now.

- If you can't afford the house you would like in the area you would like, then it **could** be the right decision for you.
- If you really want to live on a barge, then it **could** be the right decision for you—at least for now

This list could go on for pages but I won't bore you.

Decisions are based on your own experiences, feelings, the things you have heard and witnessed and perhaps a bigger picture that is holding you back or driving you forward. So what you may find is the *right move*, without really knowing every feeling, fear, hope and influence around you, others cannot really know. I have met many people who have not wanted to make the commitment of buying a house, and I understand their reasons, but at the same time, for me, it was a decision that needed no thought at all—it felt the right thing to do based on everything I have heard and how I feel when I own my home.

My priority is to be able to do what I like to my home and not have to answer to anyone else. I see a great potential to make money by owning property which is important to me—these factors may not hold any importance at all for the next person, so their decision will be based on their own reality; who am I to say it's the wrong decision? I am just another person with individual experiences and information, which gives me an alternative perspective.

My father had always stressed the importance of owning your own home—he made it look like a huge achievement, so in owning my own home, not only did I feel that my priorities had been catered for but I also had a sense of achievement in knowing that my father agreed with the decision I had made, as I respect him.

Like many others, I have viewed him over the years as an expert in many things, and this would have been an influence in my decision, or at least another drive for me to do what's *right* (for me). For other people who have not had these conversations with their family, or not had those influences, you can see how the importance may differ. I need to stress here again, that there is no wrong or right, and I wish more people would understand that their way of doing things, no matter how passionate they are about it or how much they believe it to be right, is not necessarily the next person's right way. You may like to deal with like-minded people who have similar beliefs to you, as you may respect their views, but this is not to say that other views have less importance, they might just not work for you.

Many negative people suffer from low self-esteem, resulting in a depressed mood which is often frowned upon by a 'positive person'. Optimistic and positive people want to stay well clear of these 'low-mood' people in case they are brought down by them which is completely understandable. *Low-mood* people, which I have also been known to call *mood-hoovers,* can zap the life out of you very quickly. Have you ever been feeling really positive and enthusiastic about something only to talk to someone who has a very different take on what you are saying or who doesn't share the same level of enthusiasm as you? If so, then you will be fully aware that you can soon be left feeling much less optimistic.

It's nothing new that an upbeat person can be affected by a downbeat person and sometimes these people of course should be avoided, especially if you feel that they are hindering you with their negativity. However, it is worth remembering that even the most positive people we know, sometimes have negative thoughts. Not everybody who voices a negative opinion is a negative person; they may have their own reasons for such an opinion. The people that need to be avoided the most are the people with a consistent negative outlook or approach. These negative people do not usually have much good to say about any situation or change in life, they can knock the wind out of your sail quickly, affecting your decisions and your progress.

Another reason I decided to write this book is because I want to explain positivity in greater detail.

I want people to feel that they have a chance of living a happy, fulfilled and positive life without taking every negative situation or thought as a barrier. You are not worlds apart from the people that you aspire to be like, wanting to be that happy, successful person with the perfect life balance, is not living in a dream world.

Many people who seem to have that perfect life balance and positive approach to life are often perceived as being resilient and robust, versatile and confident people who do not suffer, or have negative moments or even days. They may have that enriched balanced life that you desire so much, but that does not mean that they do not have negative thoughts or even suffer hard times, it is only human to encounter hurdles and emotions that need to be dealt with. These days, with the media looming at our every turn, it is so easy to take one perspective. Published all around us are pictures and stories, statuses and videos of how other people live their lives and want to be perceived, but the way we perceive them is not always the reality. We only really see the snippet that is shown to us. Many people do have that perfect life balance and are resilient, robust and confident but at the same time, many of these people also question their own capabilities in certain circumstances, and we don't get to hear about those moments in their lives. When we see people almost gliding through life and leaping over life's hurdles with confidence and determination, we don't always have that insight into how they really feel or what they are actually thinking. We see the actions and the snippets of what they want us to see. This is the battle that so many people have when comparing themselves to others.

If there was a speech bubble lingering above everyone's head that we walked past in the street, or who we saw on TV and social media, displaying what they are really thinking, then we would realise that we are not as far removed from the *so called* enriched, positive person as we may think we are. Even if there are differences in the thought processes, it's nothing usually that a few small tweaks and some self-belief wouldn't solve, as you will soon find out when I talk about the voice inside our heads—I'm talking about the internal monologue, (like our own commentator).

Overcoming life's hurdles

Life has many hurdles, and to overcome them you need to look at every possible angle.

Positive people also have negative thoughts, and that is something to remember when comparing or modelling yourself to someone you aspire to be like. I'll talk more about modelling ourselves later.

I have spent many hours knowing that I am a positive thinker with an optimistic approach but finding myself on this battlefield every time I was faced with a negative feeling or thought. I often told myself that I must have been kidding myself in thinking I was worthy enough to continue on my motivational journey. Fortunately for me, being surrounded by like-minded people really helped, that and a good explanation for anyone who thought that I may not be worthy of it due to a couple of areas in my life that are not picture perfect. I wouldn't even need to give any other person that explanation, as long as I had the explanation there for myself along with a filter for the negativity that may come my way. The absence of this explanation could have really held me back.

Waiting for that total perfection in my life before I felt I was worthy enough to write about it, deliver my talks and tell people my story would have meant that nothing would ever have got done.

These negative thoughts didn't hold me back, because I had my own understanding and self-belief; the understanding of how my perfection may not be another person's idea of perfection really helped me. What do you do? Keep waiting and waiting until you have reached the top and then need to go even higher because there is always someone doing *better* than you? Or wait until you have what the people around you perceive as being perfect until you take the plunge?

Ultimately, if I waited for such things, I would never have taken the plunge at all until I was running the country with a perfect network behind me, an incredible home and car, huge savings in the bank and a track record of helping thousands of people—why? Because that's what I class as being at the *top*; I'm not saying that *is* where I would like to be but it is pretty much the top from one perspective. You can see how I decided not to let a few observers that wondered whether I had it all figured out, influence my choices.

There will always be room for individual views, that's part of being a human being. Instead, I used the opinions of those who urged me to do something to help others. This filled me with the confidence to drive myself forward on this journey and even when those people are few and far between, I followed my own passion. My self-belief and passion showed me the way, alongside answering my own questioning thoughts with a positive response.

Seeing other successful people doing what I love has also helped me, but the more you follow these successful individuals that are in front of you in the hope of enlightenment and inspiration, the more hurdles you are likely to see in front of you. I say this based on the number of people I have spoken to, who have seen their idol at a fantastic workshop or presentation and left feeling very positive, only for it to last for an hour or so. When asked how they feel later in the evening, it is almost as if they are despondent or further disconnected. The feeling they had when engaging with this person is completely different to the feeling they had upon leaving the room. Some talks have left me feeling inspired forever, capturing me in a way like no other, but only the people who truly believe they are capable of climbing the same mountains will take anything positive away from it. Those who do not will only be left feeling even more inadequate, and sometimes not even aware of this shift.

The shift or change in mood is usually down to the fact that unless someone has the very same story as your own or has walked in your shoes, it is difficult to align stories. Even when you think that there are similarities, your excuses are your own, your own path is non-comparable and the information you choose to take in is not always perceived as intended. This is why, after the feeling of motivation, trepidation can sometimes follow, either that day, that week or that year, leaving a big question mark over motivational speakers and the like.

So to truly benefit from all the information that is available to you, you need to work on your own self-belief system, and I will help you with that in this book. By voicing my thoughts in situations you can see how my outcomes are heavily influenced by my thoughts and self-belief.

Many people feel that they have a special gift; they want to share their stories with you and find ways to tell you about their gift. I am not taking anything away from these fantastic people, in fact I am one. I love to tell my story; I need to write about it, advertise it and try to help others, volunteer in schools and coach people to release their full potential. There is nothing better for me than letting people know that I have had to overcome obstacles in my life, so therefore they can too. To see people transform, makes me feel that my hurdles were worth experiencing, as they have not only affected my life for the better and encouraged me to grow, but they have also helped others.

It's great to follow a path that you feel geared for; to make use of your skills and communicate your message to the world, but at the same time I see more and more people turning their life experiences into something monumental to persuade real people into spending a fortune. There are programmes and workshops to help people change their lives that cost thousands of pounds, when really, nothing is going to change if people don't understand the process. Understanding yourself and understanding the process is where the change must start from. Once you have the understanding and have nurtured your self-belief system, you can work on acquiring the knowledge that will fill any gaps in your journey.

Change doesn't come naturally to most people and this can be the hardest part of any process, because we naturally want to resist. To flip from being a negative thinker to a positive thinker isn't easy, no matter how easy people can make it look with the help of a few clichés, quotes and adorable pictures on holiday that spell out *this could be you tomorrow.*

It sounds brutal but it's the truth; change of any kind takes dedication and practice at the very least, and alongside this there are new findings and emotions to deal with. That's not to say it's not possible—in fact, it is, and that's the great news. Scientists and researchers have even proven that practice does make perfect—10,000 hours to become an expert in something to be precise, and positive thinking is no exception (blows away any theory of you either having it or not).

According to Michael Merzenich from the book 'The brain that changes itself', practising a new habit under the right conditions can change the connections between the nerve cells in our neural pathways. Neural pathways are strengthened by practise and repetition; one of the top four conditions to support this is *positive emotion.* Merzenich suggests that you start by doing something every day that you enjoy, and by focusing on that incredibly positive feeling while doing so.

I'm still grateful for all the good things in my life and every day without consciously giving it a thought, I allow this gratitude to flood in (some people call it, *counting your blessings*). It has become a part of my daily thoughts, but I do remember the first time I consciously tried to think of ten positive points in my life. Now it's ingrained and I could spend up to thirty minutes on one single point. Just thinking about one blessing leads to a whole load of positive thoughts for the day (don't get me wrong, there are other days when I spend my car journeys questioning things and trying to solve things that may not be positive, but eventually come all those blessings that keep me going, and that **"you can do it because of..."** spirit).

Many experts use a technique called *anchoring* to speed up this process which is a simple NLP technique to emphasise a particular state of mind, or mindset. You can *anchor* your own positive mindset by just realising that you are in that moment and making a mental note of how it feels. You may even decide to do more than make a mental note, and even give yourself a physical pat on the back or take a stretch.

It's all about remembering how you felt in that positive moment and being able to bring yourself back to that state at a later date by using the same *anchoring* technique. Tony Robbins uses this NLP technique in practice frequently, and breaks people's negative state within just a few minutes. People manage to recall a particular state at any given time by using anchors.

So what is anchoring?

The term 'anchoring', when used by NLP Practitioners, refers to the internal process by which the brain forms the connection.

When you were young and you had problems at school or came home sad, the arm that went around your shoulders was a display of sympathy. If you watch people's reactions when they are held in this particular way, it often resembles sadness. This is an anchor. The anchor was the arm going around the shoulder in a particular way which highlights sadness. If you are slightly down or in a space of thought and someone sits beside you, approaching you with the same display of sympathy, you feel an instant sadness as you make an association with this action.

Music is also a well-known anchor. You walk into a room and they are playing that song that you and your father danced to on your wedding day, and in a second you are there, you can feel the emotion once again (this is a replay of the emotions that you experienced at the time and not the actual emotional state you are currently in when playing the music). You may even put on a certain track when you want to feel uplifted. Some people will even choose certain music to make them feel sad, in order to think about someone or something, as a reminder or a comfort.

Anchoring is an external trigger that sets off an internal response. By consciously choosing to anchor certain emotions with certain triggers, you can then choose to recall these feelings quickly when needed.

So if you can consciously choose to anchor a feeling, like happiness, and recall this feeling whenever you chose, then why are so many people suffering for longer than necessary? Maybe more people need to be made aware of such techniques. Some people may not have the patience and dedication to learn, explore and practise, and others may not have the self-belief that they can create such positive changes (especially if their circumstances are very negative).

We are all subjected to positive and negative anchoring without necessarily being aware of it, and it's time that this technique was used more often by everyday people who it can benefit.

So how can we start anchoring and choosing when to feel happy?

1. Start by thinking of the emotion you would most like to anchor – perhaps this will be confidence.

2. Then think of an anchor that you would like to use. I used my fluffy white dressing gown as an anchor whenever I was feeling angry. It is usually used in an evening after a long relaxing hot bath when I am feeling at my most calm. When I found myself in a very frustrating argument or disagreement with my partner, and I could feel the tension rising or my anger levels increasing, I would go upstairs, throw the dressing gown over my clothes, and take 10 seconds out. Once the dressing gown was on, I could slowly feel my frustration draining away and being replaced with a much calmer and relaxed state. For self-confidence, you may choose to tuck your thumb into the palm of your hand (like another NLP expert does) each time you are in a situation that requires confidence.

3. Recall the emotion you wish to anchor and get yourself at the peak of emotional intensity.

4. Use your trigger and keep repeating.

The more you practise, the stronger the anchor will become. Practise makes perfect!

Listen to yourself

You have all the answers you need, you just need to listen to yourself carefully.

Your outlook on life (especially your own life) is voiced to yourself in a number of different ways. Listen to that voice and feed yourself with the outlook you need in order to create a better and happier life. Even if your outlook is spectacular, it doesn't hurt to refresh and check in with yourself from time-to-time, to make sure that it's still working for you.

I have always had a great outlook on life, (it's great because I check in frequently to make sure it works for me, especially after going through any changes) although I may not have always acted in the way that best represented that outlook, but the positive state has always been there. Now with life experiences and a bundle of trials and tribulations to add to my story, I can align my behaviour and thoughts with my overall outlook. It's not been an easy road getting there, but the fact is that I have learnt so much along the way and still learn to this day, striving to be a better person, both for myself and for others tomorrow. Outlooks can change when re-evaluating what works for you. Your outlook is probably not the same as when you were a child.

I am sure that I haven't experienced every emotion possible, but casting my mind back over my life, it's difficult to imagine many others. I have had, and still have, negative chitter chatter. You know, the chitter chatter that says *'I can't deal with this anymore', 'what am I doing this for', 'is this what I really want', 'you don't understand me', 'I deserve more than this', 'I'm not sure what to do'.*

You will notice that most of my chitter chatter is questioning, however, and questioning is healthy, it creates options, allowing you to reflect and evaluate.

By questioning, you are sending yourself into inquiry mode.

Epictetus, the philosopher who became famous after his release as a slave, was known for his line of enquiry, as he would question his options based on his current situation.

Epictetus was told by his master that his shackles were to be tightened to stop him escaping but he told his master that by doing this his leg would break, so it was best that his shackles were left the way they were.

The slave's master ignored his judgement and continued to tighten his shackles. The following day Epictetus's master went over to him to see what the problem was and as predicted, Epictetus's leg was broken.

The master asked Epictetus what had happened and Epictetus calmly explained that his leg was broken. Not understanding why the slave was so calm and composed, the master questioned his behaviour. The slave explained that what had been done had been done - there was nothing he was able to do about it, and by being upset or angry, nothing would change that.

The master was so impressed with the slave's attitude and reasoning that he let him go free, telling him that he must write and tell people about his philosophies, which was exactly what Epictetus did; he was quoted as saying *'it's not the things of this world that hurt us, but what we think about them'*.

You see, the way we reason with ourselves affects our outcome. The way we think and what we say in our own minds dictate whether we act positively or not. Holding on to the actual outcome that you desire the most and giving yourself time to think is the best way to get to that outcome, and that is where I have had the greatest success in my life.

You'll notice that in my chitter chatter, there were also a couple of negative statements rather than just questioning; these started with the words 'I can't' and 'you don't'. *I can't* and *you don't* are show stoppers; they are the most negative statements which show that a conclusion has already been reached. There is no room for questioning or finding a better alterative with these statements as it's a final statement. By saying 'I can't', you have already made your mind up and committed yourself to that decision. In most cases, they show *limiting beliefs,* which stop you from reasoning and being productive, beliefs such as: *even if I did do it, it would only go wrong anyway because.....*

In some cases these statements need to be made, for example, in a job that you are completely dissatisfied with, you may hear yourself say *I can't do this anymore.* That decision has surely been made after many questions. Whether you act on that decision or not, you have told yourself that a decision has been made. By not acting on that decision, you are remaining in a particular thought process which can frustrate many people, and that will continue until you either act on your decision or address yourself in an alternative way.

Limiting beliefs stop you moving forward. They are the negative beliefs about yourself that result from all that information you have taken in over the years—the story of your life, the journey you have been on and the experiences you have had.

You can turn these thoughts around. There are various ways of *re-coding* your memories and experiences by using NLP techniques, which help to drain away the negative connotations that can hinder you in life. There are also many ways that you can teach yourself to think more positively, but until you recognise these limiting beliefs, and understand the process of your own thoughts, you risk slipping back into your old negative state the moment you come close to stepping outside your comfort zone.

The truth is that everyone has fears. I met a very inspirational speaker and successful business person when on an adventure of a lifetime, and I had the pleasure of spending several days with him. We discussed the reality of life (off the stage and away from social media), a rarity for such people who spend most of their time in the limelight, and it gave me a huge insight into his/her life.

It takes trust and confidence to open up to someone, especially when you have a reputation to keep up.

Our conversations left me intrigued, and wanting to find out more about the positive role models that we have in our lives. One particular conversation we had stands out in my mind, it concerned his personal relationships. In confidence he divulged intimate details about previous and current relationships, and a story unfolded. This person, who is perceived as *having it all*, a true role model and someone to aspire to be like, in actual fact, was having a tough time of it with relationships and clearly couldn't find the love he desired. This is a normal everyday story for many people, but it was a shock to hear it of such a high profile individual who preached about life and how it should be. Not having that perfect balance in all areas of life would cast a tremendous amount of doubt in others about his role, but more importantly doubt would be cast over him. I even thought to myself, *how is this possible? You have everything, money, an amazing house, wisdom, experience, and an array of good living philosophies but yet you don't have true love? What are you doing wrong?*

I soon told myself to buck up again and to not judge, as this is just another 'normal' person with the same feelings and emotions as the next. Was I sympathising more with him because of his public status? Was I empathising with his fears of how he would be viewed if everyone knew that he didn't have love?

I soon started a different line of questioning, wondering if he really wanted to help people. *Why not let everyone know the truth so that everyone can relate? How does it really help people, showing them all the good and offering advice, if they can't truly relate? Does any motivational person actually want you to relate to them and become successful, or do they have a vested interest in people thinking that the speaker is better than the audience members, so the audience continues to buy into them?* Oh dear, the mind had started to wonder off again. *When I write my book, I want to truly help people and not be viewed as anything other than the person I really am.*

As the stories unravelled, I realised how lonely it really can be living in fear. Fear of how being too close to someone means you could risk your reputation and your livelihood (there was that social media conversation again).

By earning such sums of money, you risk falling for someone who is only attracted to the lifestyle; the fear of your partner discussing any relationship issues with friends or family. The prospect of any encounter, for him, seemed to be just as worrying, for the same reasons (and here I am—writing about it in my book). I realised that even the people we admire still have their problems and are not perfect, but what separates them from many others is the perfect understanding. After giving this much thought, I wondered how many people who find themselves in such roles, remain in unhappy relationships, just to be perceived in a particular way. Or how many people opt out of relationships entirely due to fear.

At this time I found the answers to my own life. No matter how I am perceived, for as long as I am true to myself, I am true to others. As long as we understand our choices, regardless of whether they are choices that others would also make, then we have clarity, which is all I strive for in my mind. I find solace in this when I'm not having a good day.

Another main driver for this book was to instil positivity in people and help people to realise that they can feel inspired and motivated by others without having to reach a pinnacle moment themselves in life. There is no such thing as perfection, as we all know, so there is no need to strive for it.

Focus on the things you are good at, and get help with—or delegate—the things you are not so good at. You do not need to be the one stood on the stage with stories to tell, or the multi-millionaire business person investing in each and every corner, in order to feel that you have accomplished something remarkable in life, but if that's what you want, then you, too. must understand that you can have it, or at the very least, something similar. The only thing in life working against you is the time it takes to realise it.

I was delivering a workshop a few days ago and I asked the small and intimate group to do an exercise; you can do it now if you wish. Close your eyes and imagine that you are sat in your chair as an older version of you (maybe 80 years of age) and think back over your life. Now imagine the moments you are proud of, and the memories you have.

This is an important exercise which can remind you of your core values. The way you picture your life turning out can tell you so much: what you expect to achieve, how it made you feel, the path you think you will take, and the moments you are proud of. It will also show you what you hold close to your heart, and where your real passion falls. For example, by doing this exercise, if you are currently on a business path to monetary success and material possessions, but what you envisaged when casting your mind back over your life was sadness, failings and a later life of something different, perhaps you don't have the belief you need in order to achieve that success and to continue on this path.

This exercise is a great indication of whether you are truly on the path that is right for you. I asked the group members to keep their eyes closed and keep thinking about the memories of their life in old age, but now I wanted them to think about the gifts they had used throughout their lives. Were they organised, did they touch the hearts of others, were they kind and so on? You can do the same.

One lady in the group kept opening her eyes and I could see that she was struggling with the exercise. At first I didn't know whether the group members were all capable of playing their life back to themselves (considering that we all think individually and some people don't see pictures or visualise events, they have a feeling or hear words), but it soon became apparent that she was feeling very emotional as the tears fell from her eyes.

I asked her if she was ok and she explained that she couldn't look back over her life as there wasn't anything to see. When I asked her why she thought this may be, she said that she was not happy at the moment and couldn't see anything past where she currently was. It was an emotional moment for all of us in the group as she went on to explain that she had no issue with looking back on her memories to date, but to go any further meant she drew a blank. She then explained that she knew it was because she had no idea of her path right now or how to get out of the current turmoil she was in.

It was clear to me in that moment that this exercise can show us so many things and that is why I do what I do. Try the exercise yourself and see what the results are.

When I tried the exercise, it revealed that everything I am working towards is the path I truly desire, but it also left me with a few questions about the things I didn't see that I thought were so important to me. That's given me another opportunity to delve deeper, and ask myself some more questions in order to find the reality of my thoughts. Did I not see those things because I don't believe I will have them? Or was it because I don't really want them?

It can be quite fun getting to know yourself so well. Even in turmoil, I have found this quite liberating.

The right approach

When giving my talks, I tell the tales of my biggest hurdles in life, like losing my eye or losing my 15-year-old brother to suicide. Although I don't go into any detail, I do explain how I found my path again in the face of such a diversion. I talk about how quickly life can change, but how it can also be turned around with the right channelling. We are all capable of overcoming these game changers and now, in my book, I want to tell you my stories in detail so you can really understand how. I'll be taking you with me as I reflect on this journey.

In my talks, I don't tell you about my day-to-day living and how I'm trying to create change in certain areas of my life, or how I don't have everything I desire. You, the audience fill in those missing gaps for yourself with your own judgements and thoughts based on how I have dealt with a handful of situations in my life, and even then, I you will not have the full story. Opinions are formed based on the fact that I look smart, I have arrived in an expensive car, and have the confidence to stand up in front of you with a smile and some inspirational stories. I do this to motivate you in your own life, and to help you realise that you can get through your current problems and achieve what you set out to achieve. I don't do this for you to feel inspired for an hour and then leave feeling that we are worlds apart, as I explained earlier. You gather the information from me and then make your own judgement about me according to the way you choose to process that information.

Don't get me wrong, these situations that I discuss were dealt with positively and with great optimism.

Many people have asked how I have maintained my drive and tenacity after experiencing such emotionally draining times. This sanguine approach during adversity had monumental effects on my life and contributed to the success I have today. These were the true tests for me to explore the power of positivity.

In the words of Mahatma Gandhi *'you can't change how people treat you or what they say about you. All you can do is change how you react to it'*

You also can't change certain events that happen in life but you can change how you react to them.

Your reactions are what make you responsible. These reactions are what you are judged on and lead to your *image*.

How do you imagine you are perceived?

How you feel you are perceived by others can affect your mental state, just like all that information you have taken in since birth.

If you have negative thoughts about how others may view you or feel about you, you are only contributing to your own low self-esteem, which in turn creates a closed loop.

What a person believes to be true about themselves often differs from reality, especially when talking to people with low self-esteem. This belief system is easily fed until you start to become comfortable with these beliefs. This is the danger of a *closed loop* which looks like this:

HOW A PERSON BEHAVES

HOW A PERSON SELF-TALKS

(We all talk to ourselves, either out loud, on paper or in our own minds-maybe all of the above)

A PERSON'S SELF IMAGE

So if you are always feeding this *closed loop* – you can see how important it is to be feeding it with positivity.

To create a positive thought process, you have to look at the things you are always saying to yourself and how that affects your behaviour. For example, when I wrote down my negative chitter chatter, you could see that there were a couple of closed statements like 'I can't' as I explained earlier. These thoughts are part of a self-belief system; these *show stoppers* as I call them, can have a huge impact on how we move forward, how we feel and how situations can emotionally escalate. They can cause us to act irrationally, they have no place in the mind of anyone who is unsure of the outcome they want. Show stopper thoughts will only stop you being productive, if you haven't gone through the complete questioning process.

If the truly desired outcome is to not do something anymore, then the statement 'I can't' may be welcomed. If you are saying to yourself *I can't do this anymore* when in fact, you know you have to, this thought process will serve no purpose. In this case it may be time to start coming up with some alternative messages for yourself, perhaps a line of questioning like, *I know I don't want to do this anymore so what can I do instead that will give me the result I need?*

Do you want to spend days letting this 'I can't cope' voice stand in your way, affecting how you feel? It's almost like self-harming.

I find that indulging in these thoughts is the most un-resourceful thing that I or anyone else can do; it eats away at your time, casts a negative shadow on other positive parts of your life, and limits your options, which will only make you feel worse, because it feeds that closed loop of self-doubt rather than your self-belief.

When that type of thought comes into my mind, it's the thought that comes after that makes all the difference!

Rather than just think 'I can't cope with this anymore', I instantly question why I thought that. What is the true reason? What outcome do I actually want? Will this outcome be the same tomorrow? Is there another way to do this that would make me feel happier about the situation? These thoughts are the highlighted and most constructive thoughts. It's not that I don't ever think these negative thoughts, but when they happen I try to find a positive solution.

Rather than let that one thought completely take over—which it will given the chance—I stop it in its tracks. By realising that the outcome I desire is a positive one, I soon learned to reason with myself and feel the self-pity diminish. Letting go of the self-pity and not wallowing in such thoughts can be one of the hardest things to relinquish. Sometimes you may feel like you are making headway in these moments, that you are thinking things through, but in actual fact, nothing constructive has ever come from wallowing in 'I can't'' unless followed up with a solution. You may choose to start reasoning with yourself sooner rather than later if you spend too many days thinking the same destructive thoughts.

Your thoughts will have an effect immediately, but they will also have a huge impact on your future. We all know only too well how quickly time goes. How you choose to see life determines the directions you take. If you are in a state of low-mood and have a feeling of self-pity, although quite comforting for some, you are not thinking clearly. Emotional judgement is not the same judgement you would make when feeling clear headed and balanced.

Strive to be balanced, and realise that questions, rather than negative show-stopping statements, help you to keep a balance! The answers to those questions actually create options for you.

Why would anyone want to spend any longer than one day miserable? One day is far too long; let's face it, life is short, not as short as a mayfly's, but it is certainly short for the majority of us who have endless tasks, dreams and responsibilities to deal with before we die.

If you have the control to turn things around and find alternative ways to view certain things, then do it! That part is simple. Do it, then do it again and then keep doing it. Eventually, you will do it without even thinking—in the same way that currently you can indulge in negativity without giving it a second thought.

Negativity affects us in so many different ways and it can also affect us physically; those disruptive thought processes eventually take a toll on our bodies and change our lives us if we don't get a grip of them and change them before they can do their damage. My father is a prime example of this, when he has certain thoughts about my brother (his son whom we watched disappear in a Tardis at the crematorium), his left arm goes numb, almost as if his arm, which is attached to his heart, dies each time he has to go through an emotion he is not comfortable with. This is a physical effect of his anxiety. You may have seen people who have experienced tragedy in their lives looking like it's taken its toll or perhaps you have had a tragedy yourself, or have been suffering. Life changes, routines change, thoughts change and sometimes your will to take care of yourself changes.

When you have been through a battle of emotions and some time has passed, you may reach that re-evaluation time which is crucial on any road to fulfilment. Once you re-evaluate, making a decision to care and to make the most of your time here on earth, make it a happy one, or make it happy and successful (catching those dreams you once had), then you can get to work—firstly on your thought processes.

I was reading about a nun earlier today who went blind when the church wouldn't allow her to help the community that she set out to help, after a long period of suffering and fighting for what she believed in. When she left the church and decided to help in her own way without any restrictions, her eyesight returned. You can usually see the results of long-term anxiety or depression on people's faces—not on all but on many—and this is another example of negative thoughts and stress showing themselves in a physical form.

We need to get as much happiness from this life as possible don't you think? Regardless of our story, a story is exactly what it is and *now* is what truly matters. Unless you are going to use your story to boost your morale and make positive leaps in your life, then no matter how painful it is, it's probably best either to let your story go, and focus on your now and tomorrow, or to change your beliefs of your story. You can't always change the content of what has happened but you can change the way you view it. This doesn't always take away the pain or emotion but it can make it more bearable, and can even give you the energy to alter the path you are on.

Your core values help put things into perspective. What is important to you? Is it your family and your time? Perhaps your career and the chance of promotion; could it be your faith or your peace? Or even your freedom and hobbies? Whatever you prioritise in your life will steer you in the direction that will most make you happy. When you ask your questions with your desired outcome in mind, they will be designed around your core values, your environment and your capabilities. This way you receive honest answers that work for you. When I wanted to leave my job to have flexibility and more time at home, my questions and answers were biased towards what I truly wanted. By trusting in what I wanted, I was able to work my thoughts towards making this happen. Being down and depressed about the situation I was in would not have been constructive, or given me the right energy to put my plan together.

At one stage in my life, I felt like I was dashing around like a blue-ass fly with never a moment to be still. I was doing everything for everyone else and being so conscientious, I could never say no and prioritise myself. I left myself so little time after working full time, running a business in the evenings and on my days off looking after everyone else, that I felt like I was going to break down temporarily. The only way to get any peace was to actually be ill, which rarely happened.

I had to find a solution that fitted with my core values, my environment and my actual capabilities. I questioned for a long time what I could possibly do, since everything seemed like a priority. I can't let that person down as they are just as important, I can't not help her with her shopping as she is house bound, my family needs me right now, and so on. There didn't seem to be a solution that didn't involve hurting or offending someone; sound familiar?

There are so many people stuck in that rut and struggling to please everybody while holding it together, it is no wonder so many of us are suffering deep down in silence these days, or going out of our minds in a negative closed loop. For me, I needed to come up with a solution quickly, as the novelty of doing all this good for people and being so busy had worn off about two years prior to this new-found rationale.

By keeping in mind my core values and deciding not to let my situation spiral out of control, leaving me emotionally and physically drained, I decided to alter my thought process.

Rather than feel hard done by and exhausted, I lifted my tone with a feeling of understanding for my current situation. Once I understood my situation and understood the outcome I was hoping for, I felt more optimistic about finding a solution. I had given myself time to think about what I really wanted and to define my priorities, so I came to the decision that something had to change as I was one of those priorities.

What advice would I give to a friend in this same situation? I thought. How could I get people to understand without causing offence? What compromises would help my situation? This is such a simple analysis, but one that many people struggle to complete in time before falling into a dark depression.

Whatever the situation, this analysis will help turn the situation around. You will find your own solutions when you ask yourself the right questions.

I now had all the answers I needed and the only thing left to do was act on them. Wishing I had done this a year ago, I picked up the phone the following morning and asked a family member over for coffee that afternoon. It was over that coffee that I calmly explained how I was struggling and how I was going to give myself some *me time* over the next month and cancel most commitments other than work. I was confident in my approach as I had made a committed decision. It was received well!

I then popped in to take the older lady I looked after most evenings shopping and when we arrived back at her house, as usual I unloaded the shopping and put her dinner in the oven. I would usually stay a little longer and have cake and a cup of tea, but on this occasion I explained that I was very busy and loved having tea and cake with her but I was in a bit of a rush because work was hectic and I had other commitments. Over the course of the week, I continued to do the same when popping in after work and making sure she was bathed and had clean laundry. Eventually, I felt I had eased her into understanding a little bit more about how my life was busy and how I was trying my best. I was then able to compromise and help her find someone to take her shopping at the weekends and reduce my time with her to one hour on the way home each night instead of two to four. This worked perfectly well for me and I often chose to help out for longer when needed with no pressure, because she understood. I found an alternative solution to telling her in one go which would have shocked her and made her worry. This alternative came to me after telling myself that there was no way I could tell her straight up that I was unable to help out as much. Rather than just settle for no change because it seemed impossible, I continued to search for a way, playing through all options in my mind until I found a solution I was happy with.

By taking control and realising what had to be done in order to make positive change, my life became a lot less stressful and a lot more balanced, I had more time to focus on the things I enjoyed. This was a huge turning point in my life, because even though it pivoted on such a small issue, the process gave me such huge results, that I have continued to analyse and re-evaluate. This helps to keep a balanced life, which in turn gives me the positive feeling and control that I need. Now, if something isn't working for me, I will keep trying to find a solution that fits with the outcome I want, but if there isn't a solution that I am comfortable with then a change of path may be the only way. Either way, it is a journey full of outcomes, and it should be enjoyed.

You probably already know that you must want the best outcome in order to make changes to create it. It's like the advice we are given when trying to give up smoking—*you won't give up unless you actually want to!* Sometimes what you really want though, isn't always at the forefront of your mind, and in the smoking example, it's all very well saying you don't *want* to give up smoking, but when asked if you want to be healthy, live a long life, smell better, look healthier, taste your food better, breathe easier and save more money...(you get the picture).

"To get what you want, stop doing what isn't working" – *Dennis Weaver*

I want to tell you about a terrible incident that happened when I was 21, many years ago now.

It was a normal Saturday evening and I was all ready to go out and have some fun. That night was to end in an unimaginable disaster, resulting in me being blinded in my right eye for the rest of my life.

I was in a club where a group of us danced, talked and had a few drinks, this was a normal situation for me in my late teens and early 20s. Throughout the night I was growing concerned about another woman who seemed to be very friendly with my partner at the bar—you didn't need to be a body language expert to see that there was some heavy flirting going on from her side.

I had made a couple of comments to my partner quietly over the evening and explained that I would like to leave, if he intended to continue standing at the bar with this woman and not join me with our friends. Closely watching and becoming more frustrated, I saw the woman brush my handbag away from my partner which was placed in between them on the bar and was clearly in her way. Having no control of my emotions at this stage and not being able to calmly reflect or analyse situations appropriately due to a haze of anger, I swept over to the bar and made my presence known. I forcefully placed my hand on the woman's shoulder and the other around her hair. I can recall what went through my mind at the time: *I want to get out of here but why should I, she should leave, look at her in her little skirt, she doesn't even care that I'm here, I'll show her how far she has pushed me now.* Clearly this wasn't the way to go about it and by the time I had applied more force on her shoulder—which happened in a matter of three seconds—I had been glassed. The woman had smashed her wine glass on the side of the bar and drove the stem into my face—a reaction I would not have anticipated in a million years.

The gushing of negative thoughts that had rushed through my mind that evening was to have its consequences. The negative thoughts led to poor decision making and behavioural changes. In order to have acted differently, I would have had to feel differently, and in order to have felt differently, I would have had to alter my thought processes. Everything stems from the way we perceive a situation, but that's just hindsight now.

I do not regret my actions that evening, as it was a life changer for me. They have led to the person I am today, and the understanding of myself and the people that I now have around me. I question whether I would have the wisdom I do now, without this sequence of events. I was always a kind and caring young girl, but I made a few silly mistakes when letting my thought processes get the better of me. This particular mistake proved to be the biggest I could have made.

For me, all those years ago, it was normal to have negative thoughts in such a situation, thoughts like:

'I feel lonely, and I am not being respected now'

'I cannot believe you are acting this way, you deserve to be punished'

'It seems that he likes her more than me'

'I would never act like that, so why is she. Who does she think she is?'

These thoughts may seem childish and insecure now, but it's not so much these initial thoughts I would have a problem with, it's the previously absent follow-up thoughts that have changed situations in my life now. The questions I have been speaking about throughout this book, that we should ask ourselves, change outcomes; along with understanding why we have such thoughts? The answer to that question can unravel a lot of mystery.

My story was published in local newspapers and nationwide magazines, but never once did anyone write about how it had initiated, because that wouldn't have told a story that people wanted to read about. I was told that people only wanted to read about the poor victims, and what a dreadful place the world can be at times. I didn't even want people to know the entire truth about that evening because it would paint me in some awful light, however, having learnt so much over the years, I am glad to be able to tell you.

It wasn't the case that I was dancing and stepped on her toes accidentally, or that I got caught up in a brawl or even in the wrong place at the wrong time as many press releases stated (not that I told them, that but it's what they made up to keep people interested). That isn't what happened: my thoughts are what happened, which were soon to be followed by my emotionally led actions.

I didn't deserve that outcome in my mind, and I never thought that people were capable of such actions like smashing a glass and using it in such a way, but I learnt the hard way.

If I had questioned these initial thoughts such as 'It seems that he likes her more than me' with a rationale such as: *Does talking and laughing with someone at a bar suggest he likes her more than me, the person he lives with?* I would have been able to answer logically. By applying a rational thought process, and understanding the reality of each thought, you are more likely to get a grasp of your emotions and less likely to act in an inappropriate manner or even to become introverted as a result of your thoughts.

You see, as a younger woman, I didn't have much control over strong emotions and negative thoughts. Although mainly upbeat, bubbly and smiley, I still had trouble dealing with anything negative. I had escalated this situation in my mind subconsciously, affecting my ability to deal with each situation appropriately and to give me the outcome I desired.

Whilst lying on the floor, covered in blood and waiting for an ambulance, I was unaware of the extent of my injuries. I could feel that it was bad but being an optimist, I thought I needed to get fixed up quickly before work on Monday and was more concerned about how I was going to get to hospital, if this ambulance didn't hurry up—along with just wanting to go to sleep (that's more to do with being in shock than anything else).

Kindly, the bouncer of the next pub took me to the hospital in his car. I am sure the fact that an ambulance was not available for a number of hours was something to do with the volume of Saturday night poor decision making (especially when under the influence of alcohol).

Lying in hospital with the stem of the glass still protruding from my eye socket, I watched the wonderful people all around me; my family that had rushed to my bedside and all the staff that waited on me hand and foot in their empathetic state. I had an overwhelming sense of appreciation for these people at this time and knew I had their support. With time to think overnight as I waited to be operated on, I wondered what on earth had just happened to my face. The excruciating pain had only just begun.

I knew I would be very lucky to walk away without any scars, and I also knew that there was a chance that my eye had been damaged permanently, although at this time, losing an eye was not really something I had considered.

After conversations with doctors and nurses, I was able to start building a picture of what had just happened. Even though I hadn't been given any solid information, I had to start preparing myself for the loss of an eye. Shocked and deeply upset, I started to feel bitterness and anger. I held my partner responsible during this time and refused to see him in hospital. Hurt and distraught, my partner went through turmoil in the hospital waiting room.

After many hours, I agreed to see him and it was in that moment that I forgave him instantly. Realising that none of this was his fault by thinking rationally and not just reacting emotionally, I could see his pain and intent clearly. It didn't change the event or the aftermath but it meant there was hope for a better future. With everyone's support, I went in for my long operation. I could see the dread, fear and sadness on everyone's faces as they rolled me down to theatre, and I decided that I would remain optimistic in the hands of such a wonderful surgeon who had already spoken to my father, telling him that he would treat me just like one of his daughters, and do the very best he could to leave as little visible damage as possible. I felt comfortable and in safe hands. I told them all that I would be just fine and that there was nothing to worry about!

Many hours later after my surgeon had performed a very complex operation, managing to stitch my eye back together and saving the muscles that he could, I woke up in recovery. I was so elated to see, I was once again filled with emotion and more grateful for sight than I have ever been in my life. Sight was never something I took for granted anyway, it was one of those gifts in life that I took time to appreciate on many occasions, but that day, there was a new sense of gratitude. Rather than feel the loss of an eye, I felt I had gained an eye—it was as though I had just been given sight for the first time.

How could I possibly remain bitter and resentful when I was so lucky to be able to see all this beauty around me?

I instantly wanted to go home and return to work, and get on with life with my new sense of appreciation, but life doesn't always work in the way you expect. Instead, I was bombarded with tests. The tests would give the doctors an indication of how successful the operation was and the extent of the damage. After test number one, I was convinced that all was going to be fine and that I would be able to see again sometime soon in the near future, the fact that I could see all the colours they were asking me about was a good sign, right? The problem was that my mind was imagining these colours. I had got all the colours wrong and not once did any of the staff let me know, until all tests had been completed. Sat there in (literally) blind optimism, I was told that I had identified the colours incorrectly and hadn't actually seen any light through my eye.

I couldn't believe it, my heart fell through my stomach when I realised that this had only been in my imagination (I needed some serious convincing). I then told myself that I was blind in that eye and I would do whatever I could to make it better, but I had to come to terms with it.

I got up to take another look in the mirror and staring back at me was a mosaic of black and blue bruises. *One step at a time* I thought, *this is not going to be a case of returning to work on Monday and forgetting all about it.* I didn't even recognise myself.

My workplace was then contacted and I knew, as did they, that this was going to be a long journey. I wanted to do whatever I could to make it as short as possible and return to normality. I knew this was my goal, and any hurdles would have to be dealt with when they came along, as I could never have foreseen all the issues I would face. I felt equipped with only the determination to be happy again and to minimise its intrusion in my life as much possible.

When my manager came to visit me, he told me that I would no longer be able to drive again, and as my role was a field sales consultant, this meant I would not be able to retain my job. Another big hurdle had just landed on my doorstep!

The staff members at my workplace were very supportive, but after hearing that I would only be entitled to statutory sick pay, and that my company car had to be returned along with my expenses buffer of £200 that was initially paid in to my bank account when I joined the company, I could see that things were not going the way I was expecting.

It all made me feel like I could easily fall into a deep depression. Fortunately for me, the prospect of this scared me. I could sum it all up in less than a minute: if I don't do what it takes to get better soon, and show everyone that I can do the things I used to do, then I will definitely lose my job, lose my income, lose my independence, possibly my house, and more importantly my happiness. That was easy, then, there was only one thing for it: don't get depressed; do whatever it takes methodically to get better, and get back on track, just as I had told myself at the very start of this. I didn't know exactly what that consisted of, but I knew I had made a commitment to myself, and that the best way to start was to get a plan together.

To avoid depression meant that I had to stay positive and look at everything as a new challenge that needed to be faced in order to achieve my longer term goal; I had made peace with that approach.

My peace didn't last long. Soon I started to fall into deep depression, and it felt as though I had any control of it. All I had to do was look in the mirror, it didn't seem to matter what I thought about, or how determined I was to get this right, I still felt miserable and out of control. It lasted two days and that was enough to give me a taste of what I had to look forward to if I remained depressed. Being depressed wasn't an easier option for me long term at all, so I had to get a grip of myself and understand what would lift me out of this dark state.

Through the interrogation I gave myself, I found my answers. I could no longer compare how I used to look to how I looked now as there was nothing I could do about that. I was released from this awful state of depression in just 48 hours and I felt quite impressed by myself. I could feel everything change, having experienced what I didn't want to become. This experience of sheer misery was enough to remind me of what life could be like if I didn't adapt.

I could recall this state of depression whenever I needed to, as a reminder of what I didn't want to become. I would later use this as a reminder of the reason why I was soldiering on, and trying to overcome each challenge I faced when things got a little tough, or when my energy was depleted.

My biggest issue now was finding a way to overcome each challenge—the challenges that were possible to overcome. The ones I had no control over, like my appearance, I couldn't change, so there was no point in focusing on them (I could, however, make small improvements by taking care of my wounds and using oils to soften the scars. Taking care of myself gave me some pleasure).

Being methodical, I realised that the most important thing here was money, which I needed in order to keep everything ticking over as usual, and to maintain the lifestyle that I was happy with before the accident. This may not be the priority for some people and I hear now, even when writing this, the number of times people will say, 'money isn't everything' and 'health is more important'. This I believe to be true, but money is a close second to me, because with money you have options, and at least when your bills are being paid, you do not carry such burdens.

With health, you are free to earn and have the privilege of options. I had health, I was just injured but with no pay-out (even after several appeals). My mental health would have been even more affected if I had been under any more pressure; not having a job or money would lead to bills not being paid, which would have had more of a detrimental effect on my mental health than working hard to get my life back on track. This I was sure of.

I was persistent in voicing my desire to come back to work as soon as possible, but my employers were adamant that I needed time to heal. I understood what they were saying, and their empathy was appreciated, but that wasn't helping me financially. After looking into all my options, including temporarily receiving some benefits to bridge the gap, I decided that remaining on the payroll and not receiving benefits would suit me better. I now needed to make sure that I overcame my employer's main objection to me coming back to work so soon which was my ability to drive again. There was only one thing for it, and that was not to let other people's opinions of me affect my own opinions of myself.

I needed to get back in a car and drive again. I demanded that I my company car was returned. As I had paid tax on a company car and there was no legislation in place to say that I couldn't drive, it was just a matter of declaring it and going through any necessary tests to prove my competence. I was sure they couldn't argue with this if it was put to them in the appropriate way. I later had an older pool car delivered to my door.

While all this was going on, my father and I were running a shatter-proof glass campaign to make drinking in pubs safer. Interviews and radio shows were filling my dad's diary, and he insisted on protecting me from all the letters and phone-calls that kept coming in. I helped where possible, and I was the face of the campaign but my dad was out there every day getting those signatures on the petition which finally went to parliament. The legislation was passed, and today when you drink from those sturdy shatter-proof glasses or plastic beakers and bottles, you will understand why.

Just as in Epictetus' tale, *what had happened had happened and nothing could change that, but I was in control of what could happen next and the best person to create that change for me, was me.*

I was offered counselling which, at the time, I could see no benefit in. I was on a mission to make things right again myself. I had a plan of action and a bucket full of determination, so talking about what had happened, why it had happened and how I was feeling, was only going to hinder me. I decided to decline any offers of counselling at this stage and that I would re-evaluate in the future, if I felt I needed any help. I didn't close the door to it, I just put it on the back burner for the time being, in the knowledge that I was in a positive place and I couldn't risk changing that for any reason.

'Let's hope I wake up with the same level of enthusiasm in the morning' I told myself. In that moment it dawned on me that I had complete control of this situation and all my actions were going to make a difference. Living in *hope* that I wake up in the same mind-set tomorrow was not going to be enough to make change; I had to KNOW it, I had to make sure of it, and not settle for anything less.

How many times do you find yourself in situations where you hope you will feel ok, or hope something works in your favour? You have more control than what you often realise or give yourself credit for.

I could not allow myself the opportunity to have a bad day and feel low, I had a lot to do, and a lot to prove to the people who would help me make that difference I needed. Sitting around feeling sorry for myself was not going to make anything better and I was fully aware that such emotions could spiral out of control, considering the extent of the damage that had already been done. I decided that if I was feeling fragile at any time, I would allow myself some comfort time, to reflect and remain positive; to rest and be still; but not time to wallow. I made a committed decision to keep moving forward, and a rest day from time-to-time would help me move forward—especially if I had earned it.

At 7.00 a.m. the following morning I awoke to the loud sound of the alarm that would usually wake me for the day's work that lay ahead. It was a familiar sound. No job to go to, nevertheless, a lot to do. Much had changed but there I still needed an element of routine to embark on the missions ahead.

Changing my dressings and bathing my wounds, taking tablets to ease the pain and answering the phone to a number of people who relied on updates to relieve their concerns took priority most mornings. I found myself consoling friends and family, telling them that I was going to be ok and that there was nothing that I needed. The visitors kept coming and before you know it, another day had nearly passed!

I'd ask myself at the end of each day that went like this: *'what have I actually achieved today'*

Soon I started to feel trapped and miserable. There wasn't enough productivity and progression to continue to sustain my enthusiasm yet I didn't seem to be to blame for that. I couldn't fit anything else into a day and the days were running away from me far too quickly. Realising that by the time I had spoken to everyone and updated people that I had no time left to actually make any real progress, I had yet another decision to make to create another change in the way I was doing things. I had to be slightly stronger in my approach with the people that surrounded me.

By questioning why I felt so miserable at the end of each day after having woken up in such a motivated state, I was able to get to the bottom of the issue. Rather than just stay in a state of 'feeling', I wanted answers and solutions to alleviate the misery.

Surrounding yourself with the right people at the right time in your life is crucial. This is why so many people tell you to stay away from negative influences and only bring in closer the positive types. I don't believe that it is as clear cut as that. Sometimes, people can have a positive outlook but still hold you back. When I set out on my path, committed to a particular journey, it's with the greatest respect that I choose who I engage more with. In this case, the people around me were not to be completely cut off because of negativity, in fact they were just caring, considerate and positive people, but their energy was stifling me. The amount of time I dedicated to them was affecting my progress, and their consideration was not as helpful as they intended, so I was left with no other alternative than to explain exactly that, as diplomatically as possible. Essentially I was telling them I needed to be left alone, and that they had to trust in me enough to know I was going to be ok.

I compromised and said I would call frequently, but only when it was convenient for me. The message was loud and clear so I think everyone understood, but regardless of whether they did, it was another committed decision made, that would help to get me back on track. Empathy is great, but too much can sometimes bring you to a state of apathy. I was not prepared to even get close to that.

These small decisions in life can have the greatest of impacts.

Back in the car

The car was on the street outside my house and I was itching, however nervous I was, to get in it and feel my independence again. After insisting that my partner went back to work, he eventually agreed; his parting words before leaving in the morning were 'Now don't go and do anything stupid like go off in the car without me, you have to be patient and take things one step at a time.' *Ah, ok then*

Gripping the steering wheel as tightly as possible and taking about 15 minutes to check that my mirrors were located in the optimum position, I gently squeezed down the accelerator.

Pulling off from the street and carefully driving down the tight road with cars parked on each side, it dawned on me that this was all guess work. What was I thinking? I couldn't even pour the hot water into a cup for a coffee in the morning without creating a flood across the kitchen floor; perception was not my strong point now. Having reached the end of the road, I sat lingeringly at the give way sign. When I saw a car eventually approach in my rear-view mirror, without haste, I pulled away. Now on the main road and with my heart pounding through my chest, I reminded myself, that I was only going to the shops. It is, without doubt, one of the scariest moments in my life. I had underestimated the responsibility I would feel, not to mention the huge visual black spot I had. Taking it slowly, I finally arrived at the supermarket where I parked the car and turned the engine off as quickly as possible, deep breaths and watery eyes marked the moment of achievement.

It didn't seem like a big achievement driving 10 minutes across town to a local supermarket, in fact, I was disappointed in how draining it actually was. After I had calmed down and re-focussed, I was ready for a good shop and maybe a little treat, but yet again there was to be more fear that I hadn't accounted for. Everything just kept sweeping in to surprise me, more and more little hurdles raised their ugly heads, trying to pull me back. What I thought was going to be a trip out to get back to normality turned in to some exhausting experience that I never wanted to repeat again.

With the trolley, I froze and all confidence diminished.

I had only travelled down one isle and there I was, guilty of the bottom shelf products rolling around the floor. Collecting all the glass jars and putting them back on the shelf, a lady made a comment and laughed supportively and then I turned around; the look of horror on her face was a picture that remained firmly engraved in my mind for the rest of that day. I can't really picture it now but for about a year afterwards, it was so vivid. I had forgotten the severe state my face was in. No right eye to look at (or at least one that has shrunk and is bright blue), scars all over the right hand side of my face and bruising that you could probably see from the other side of the shop, let alone stood there right in front of me. I gave her a consoling look as if to say *'Don't worry; I'm sorry if I startled you.'*

After bumping into people, display stands and trolleys, I froze in the middle of the isle. I had barely finished picking up the jars from my last escapade, what on earth would be next? Everyone was staring and I was feeling more and more trapped in this isle. No one to call and no way of getting out other than walking past all these people was a suffocating thought. I turned and faced the cereals when I heard a man's voice 'cheer up love, it might never happen' *mmmmm* I thought, *it already has idiot.* Walking quickly through the store, leaving my trolley abandoned next to the cereals, I jumped back into my car and burst into tears. I never expected things to be this hard. The simple tasks in life had turned into monumental events.

What am I going to do?
You can't just sit here.
You can't leave your trolley in the isle for someone else to unload.
How am I going to get home? I am so shaken up!
I was told to stay at home, maybe I should have.
I'll call someone and get collected! If I do that then they will all keep an even closer eye on me and make sure that I don't get back in the car again anytime soon. You mustn't show this weakness, you must complete the day.

Once you complete the day and get home, you will feel
much better and you'll have your shopping.
I'm not used to people looking at me in this way though, it
must be awful to look strange permanently to be stared at,
I hope this bruising and scarring goes away soon. Maybe I
should get a patch to cover it up so it's not so shocking to
other people. I wonder if the supermarket sells a patch.
That's what I'll do; I'll go back and get my trolley, buy a
patch and make my way back home to relax.

That was pretty much all my thoughts when sat in the car.
I smiled and went back in. My trolley was still in the same
place, so I just continued from where I left off. Five hours
later: 'how was your day?' my partner asked. 'Eventful' I
replied with half a smile.

Only then could I look back and smile with that sense of
achievement. I had been through a lot that no one else
was really aware of. I explained that I had been to the
shops in the car and that everything was fine, apart from
being a little scary, with a couple of frozen moments in the
supermarket that didn't involve buying ice-cream. I
decided not to mention it to anyone else at this stage, I
would just say that I had a good and productive day.

Tomorrow I was going to get on the motorway. Most of my driving for work was motorway driving. I thought I would feel more comfortable with it as there didn't seem to be so many hazards to look out for. This big blind spot wasn't an issue once you learnt to turn your head around 180% quickly and use your mirrors twice as much. I was now that annoying driver who takes much too long to pull away at a roundabout, but that was just how it had to be, and everyone else would just have to learn to be a little more patient and forgiving.

The motorway went well; I had now driven a total of an hour and was feeling a lot more at ease with the process. I had my new pirate patch on, and I decided that it wasn't really me. I preferred people to stare and understand the problem rather than not know what the problem was but stare just as much anyway. I was finding my feet in my new situation.

Refusing to have a prosthetic lens was a hard decision but it was a decision I made regardless. So many people couldn't understand why I wouldn't want something that made me look 'normal' again. I wasn't quite ready for it yet anyway as my stitches hadn't been removed.

I couldn't open my eye due to the swelling but it was an offer that was being spoken about. It scared me, I thought it would confirm that I had lost my sight in that eye if I went ahead and covered it up with a lens. I still had this strange sense of belief that my sight would come back, and if I was to cover up my eye with a prosthetic lens, I would be resigning myself to this blindness; *my eye wouldn't have to try and work anymore so it would just fall asleep for ever* – It was like giving it permission to die.

I wanted my eye to continue to try and work, so that if there was any possibility that my sight could come back, I had given it the best shot I could. This meant that I refused to have a prosthetic lens for six months. You could call it denial but I was fully aware of my current situation, I just didn't want to give up on any little hope I had just yet.

Back to work

After a holiday and a few extra trips in the car, I was back at work. At first they had said that they couldn't insure me for the vehicle any longer and that I needed to prove somehow that I was competent enough. With that, I booked a mobility driving school test; it was great, it certified me as a competent driver, in fact, they said that my perception was now better than most of the average drivers they assess. Happy with this news, I drove in to work and handed my manager the certificate. He praised me for my sheer determination to get back to work and welcomed me back with huge open arms.

The £150, when not being paid was a bit of a sting, but everything now had become worth it. Every lost penny, every tear and every hurdle was suddenly a satisfying memory; this was the moment I had been waiting for: my goal, the outcome I desired.

Working with goals is so important, I was aware that there would have to be other goals along the way but this was an achievable goal; it was a realistic outcome that wasn't too far in the future that it would ever feel unachievable, perhaps difficult, but not unachievable. Within one month, I had been on holiday and got my job back after experiencing such a terrible ordeal. I thanked my goal setting for this and the support I had around me. Everyone was proud. I had overcome all the objections that my employers had raised about me joining the team again, and now I had the confidence to do the same with all other goals I set myself.

I usually call it an accident as it was something that should never have happened. Earlier in the book though I referred to it as an incident as it wasn't an accident, it was an intentional act on both sides but the outcome for me was not intentional. Maybe it should be called an incident but whatever you chose to call it, I didn't expect that outcome.

A new eye

We are all sales people, whether we are in sales as a career or not, we are all aware of how to sell something; whether that is selling yourself, a product or a service, we are all able to sell something. As a sales person we are taught to sell professionally in order to get the result we want or need at the end of the process. By asking open questions, you give an opportunity for all areas to be explored and elaborated on, thus finding a solution a lot easier. Open questions which cannot be answered with just a yes or no are a fantastic way to fact-find and understand objections. It still amazes me how many people are capable of asking these open questions to others but yet struggle to ask themselves such questions.

It's these open questions that I constantly ask myself, because they help me reach my goals and find the result I am looking for. With this level of questioning, life moved faster forward for me and before I knew it, I was running my own business, buying a big detached house and taking lots of amazing holidays. I never would have guessed when lying in that hospital bed that I would go from strength to strength at a much faster pace than I ever had before.

As always, there were issues along the way, like facing the public in meetings with a disfigured face, seeing their discomfort when talking to me. The questions people would ask me like, 'were you in a car accident?' The looks people would give me as if I was a victim of some domestic abuse were tough to take at times and this was something that I was struggling to find a solution for. The bruising had gone but the scars remained. It didn't seem to matter how much I told myself that it didn't matter what other people thought, it didn't seem to help. I still managed to attend all of my meetings and meet new people but I just didn't feel the same person. Eye contact had become a struggle and sitting too close to someone suddenly felt very awkward. I had to keep putting myself in these situations in order to keep my job and to run my business, but I wanted to find a way that would make it more comfortable for me. I remembered the conversation about the prosthetic lens and after receiving a large anonymous donation of £25,000; I thought it was time to sit down and give this some serious thought.

The letter that had come with the donation had made it clear that the money was to be used for the best private treatment I could find and advised that I perhaps go to America. The letter mentioned plastic surgery which scared me very much. I had just got my life back on track and wasn't feeling too great about the idea of taking more time off work, going abroad for treatment and entering into the unknown world of plastic surgery. I was starting to get used to my new face and that would mean more upheaval that I didn't think I was ready for. After days of thinking, I decided to give the donation back. However, I realised that having two similar eyes again would be a welcome look. It was a wonderful feeling that somebody watching the news had gone out of their way to make such a donation to me to help me get my life back on track. Such a warm and generous gesture for a stranger to make. It felt almost wrong to give the money back, but at the same time, I didn't want to use it for what they intended, so it was the right thing to do.

The NHS did an amazing job; appointment after appointment, some discomfort and a while to wait but I got there, my first prosthetic lens was ready to wear as little or as often as I liked. I loved it! It took a while to get used to and at first it felt like putting a brick in my head but I soon grew used to the feeling and it became a part of me, in fact, something that I would become dependent on. It was great to see a more symmetrical face again that didn't leave every person I met with a list of questions they wanted to ask me. Some people still insisted on finding out more when they could see that something wasn't quite right but as my surgeon had managed to save the muscles, I was lucky to have movement with my new eye. The lens would move as it was placed on top of the shrunken existing eye. Now I just looked like I had a lazy eye from time to time, I could deal with that.

There were a number of mixed emotions that came with my new eye and I was aware that I was now dependent upon it. I could no longer attend a meeting without it, not even open the front door to the postman.

It had become a part of me and I was so scared of losing it. It's not as if you can just quickly get another one made. The endless appointments and skill that had gone into this amazing prosthetic meant it couldn't just be replaced. I had to protect it in every way I could – it had now become my independence. It felt like it was me—well, it was me to the outside world—when I was home, I took it out to avoid discomfort.

It would have been impossible to have positive thoughts throughout the entirety of this process. There were many mixed thoughts but getting a positive outcome meant having to go through all of these thoughts to find the positive solution I was looking for. It wasn't easy getting to know a new face, but constantly comparing my new face to my previous face was not getting me anywhere, so in order to feel positive I decided not to compare, and to be grateful for the technology that has helped me aesthetically.

Changing direction

Years had passed and I had changed direction completely. Discovering how life can throw the unexpected at you at a time when you least expect it, I decided to make some changes in my life.

Changing direction isn't always easy, especially when you have worked very hard at something and are unsure of whether you will get the result you want, but some things are very clear: when making a complete change of direction in your life, you need to be clear about the path you are choosing, or at least what that path entails in the beginning. We don't always know where exactly that path is going to end up but if we can have a clear indication of what to expect from it and the exact steps that are necessary to start, then we have a much better chance of making the desired changes.

Start small and keep focused on what you want.

I had opened myself up to all the possibilities that lay in front of me and was no longer prepared to stay focused on where I had been and what I had done for so long. I wanted something new and exciting, a new challenge, and a chance to explore who I wanted to be. I didn't want to just be the girl living with the accident I had been through and clinging on to everything I knew, including my partner because I was scared of anything new.

It had become easy for me to tick by each day feeling secure and safe around all the people who I knew and who had helped me through such a traumatic time in my life. I wasn't completely aware at the time of making these changes why I wanted the change but I had a feeling that was unexplainable; it was an urge to change direction completely and follow the unknown. Even with so much good surrounding me like a great husband (we had got married a year after my accident and had been happy for 10 years), my business, the house and the car. Jumping out of my comfort zone became my greatest passion. That however, came with its own consequences, but they were consequences that I had expected. I was growing in a different direction that didn't suit the lifestyle I was leading anymore, so I felt that whatever the consequences were, I had to make the changes.

I had a huge amount of fun, and experienced lots of new things physically and mentally when I made my changes, which led to an all-round important growth that I was subconsciously searching for, but there was heartache and pain along the way too.

The change led to me hitting rock bottom when the path I felt I had mapped out wasn't quite as I expected. That feeling of having lost everything decided to kick me in the stomach a couple of years later once it had all gone wrong. I was in a place which felt so open and lonely but looking back now, it only contributed to where and who I am today and that is what I am grateful for in life. In all those moments, I never wished to have back all I had known before and by understanding myself the way I do today, I am able to reflect on this and realise that the positive thoughts I still had, even when the plan had failed, was what continued to feed my self-belief.

There is not a decision I regret, and as a coach and NLP therapist now, I have joined a network of people who hold the presupposition that there is no wrong or right decision, only decisions that allow us to grow and develop, learn and discover (unless you are breaking the law of course). I had done what I wanted to do, and more importantly, what I believed I could do, so having done it, I knew I could do it again, I just needed to know what I wanted to do.

If you think you can do a thing, or think you can't do a thing, you are right – Henry Ford

There are no right or wrong decisions in life, as long as you're not breaking the law—only experiences that we learn from. We are constantly learning and taking in information, so everything contributes to that journey of ours. I am sure you have experienced a number of trials and tribulations of your own, perhaps heartache and loss of a loved one or maybe loss of the material things in life that you have worked so hard for. Overcoming any of these hardships can be tough, and at the time it can be very hard to see any light at the end of the tunnel. I was once told to think about where I was five years ago; I did that and was then asked if I was going through anything in my life that I was struggling with around that time. I was then told to try and remember how I felt and whether I believed I would come through it, and be in a better place. Did I get through it? Am I in a better place? Then I was asked to think back to five years before that, where was I then? Did I overcome those moments in my life that, at the time, I had such little faith in overcoming?

You can do the same. Think back five years! Where were you? Were you facing any hurdles? If yes, try to remember how you felt. So why, when faced with new hurdles, do we sometimes doubt our resilience– Sometimes it feels like the end of the world but you're here to tell the tale, and hopefully a much better one than you would have told five years ago. Now go back a further five years. Look at how good you are at overcoming issues. Whether you dealt with it in the way you would now or not is irrelevant, what's relevant is that you got through it and you can get over the next hurdle too, especially with all the experience you have gained during those last ten years. Although this seemed like quite a simple tool, it made a lot of sense and actually helped me.

There are so many examples of extraordinary people who have made unbelievable changes in their lives against all odds.

Recently I read about a man who was paralysed and unable to communicate. The breakthroughs he made by holding on to the possibility of a positive outcome were outstanding. What some people call a miracle others call the power of a positive mental attitude. He didn't stay in his hospital bed for months believing that there was no hope, but instead had been thinking of ways to create change, exploring all avenues of possibilities. Eventually he found a way to communicate with the help of the experts around him, managing to convey his message.

Going from strength to strength, he was able to help others in the same situation, and became an incredible influence in making such communication possible today. What an achievement for someone who was actually unable to communicate themselves at one stage. Moving forward with his new methods of communication, he was then able to indicate what he wanted and needed, leading to a much more fulfilled life that they embraced regardless of the issues he had, which many would find difficult to cope with.

When we are thrown into these life changing situations, often it's a case of sink or swim, so from an outsider's perspective, it may look like the person involved is taking everything in their stride and the thought of you being in that same situation is daunting. Perhaps you think you wouldn't be able to approach such life-changing things with the same amount of positivity but when you actually break it down and you realise that you do actually have a choice, it soon seems like a `no-brainer'. Move forward or not – I bet you chose to move forward. People may think they would chose to move forward but by not making the committed decision to actually alter their thought processes or break down exactly what needs to be done in order to 'move forward', you don't actually move anywhere. Instead you stay in a stagnant pool of water where you remain treading water until you have had enough and decide to do something serious about it.

Just when you think you're on track

This crazy life doesn't want to let things run smoothly for too long for some of us. No, it wants to remind us that we have to stay on our toes; that's what I think now when looking back over my life's events. Just when you and your family thought you had been dealt your fair share of bad luck, there seemed to be more.

No matter how much heartache and pain you have already felt, nothing prepares you for that dreaded phone call, the one that will change your life, and possibly your outlook.

I got that call. Saturday morning and there I was setting up a craft stall with my mum in Wales. We were hoping for a good day with lots of sales, the mood was bright and cheerful. Realising that my phone battery was almost depleted, I left my phone charging on the other side of the hall. There was a bounce in my step that morning. A huge smile was a complete giveaway to my mum that I was feeling happy. My new house had gone through and I was in the middle of a brand new renovation project. It was the first house I had owned on my own with complete control over what I did with it and when. My creativity had gone wild. A huge sense of freedom had swept over me and after all the heartache I had been through when I changed direction and the path had not been as expected, I felt liberated and free; the hard work had all paid off. I felt so happy, I voiced it to my mum.

From an emotional wreck who cried herself to sleep night after night in complete despair due to a relationship breakdown, I managed to work on the tasks ahead that I had set myself to build my life back up. I did it! Well I knew I would, I had past experience in putting my mind to something and getting the result I needed. It was that proof that kept me going. I was finally reaping the rewards again. It had been a long road and had taken some persistence through tough times but I was finally there, living with peace—or so I thought!

I didn't want any more changes in direction, I knew now what I wanted, and I was on track to getting it while enjoying my incredible journey.

Mum gave me that look which spoke a thousand words, 'You've done so well and I can see that you are happy, but wouldn't it be lovely if you had someone to share it with and even a family of your own?' She didn't have to say anything, looking over at the magazine Perfect Family positioned to the left of us, I got it!

I knew that was next. I had my doubts how and when exactly but with so much to focus on right now, I had a lot to do and enjoy. I wanted this roll to continue.

I loved listening to that song *ain't nothing gonna break my stride, ain't no one gonna slow me down woooa nooo, you've got to keep on moving.*

Twelve missed calls from dad? That was unusual for sure. *He must have sold something at the motorhome show he's at! Oh, and he'll be very excited about it. Actually, I hope everything is ok, it's strange how he has called so many times.* Mum hadn't spoken to dad for years, they got divorced when I was very young, I lived with my dad growing up as a single child until he met someone else when I was nine. They married and she became my step-mum. Not an unusual story, although there are lots of unique stories I could bore you with. I won't, but just to confuse you, I call both of the women in my life 'mum'. I was blessed to have a new family, although as a teenager, it probably never came across like that. A step sister, who is like a biological sister to me, (she was three when they got married and we all moved in together), and a further two children that mum and dad had after marrying. Another younger sister and then a brother followed. Dad finally had his boy and we had a great team, a beautiful family.

I explained to mum (biological mother) that I thought something strange was going on and that I had to go and make a call to dad as I had 12 missed calls. Looking worried, I walked out to the car park; I had no idea that strange something could turn out to be quite as devastating as it was (still is).

Dad was squealing something down the phone at me but I couldn't quite hear him. Did he just say Callan's dead? No, my ears must be playing tricks on me. He sounds like he's laughing. He sounds like he's in a car when he should be at the show selling. I don't understand. All I could do was repeat myself, "What did you say Dad?" There it was again, "Callan's dead." I had to repeat what he said for confirmation but I could barely get the words out myself. Through the howling that was coming from the end of the phone, I said 'Dad, did you say......?' Suddenly, silence as I repeated his words then a quiet and weak 'yes' made its way from my dad's mouth. I can't believe I actually asked if he was joking, but it just couldn't be true, there must have been a mistake, as obviously, there would never have been such a joke. "Dad, where are you?" I cried from the pile of mess I had become on the concrete floor. My legs had gone to complete jelly and my *yelps* must have been heard as people flocked out through the hall doors. I wanted everyone to go away and for this floor to open up and drag me under. "I'm in the back of a police car," Dad explained. That was the extra confirmation, now I really knew that this was actually happening. I had a million things going through my mind, the first thought was that my brother must have been hit by a car and that really, he was going to be ok and that Dad just hadn't been given the good news yet. That thought didn't last long.

Mum picked me up off the floor and frantically shouted at me. I think she was asking what was going on and what had happened. "Give me the phone" she shouted in a bid to help, as no one could understand a word I was saying. I just shouted at her that I needed to go home. She needed to get me home, but home was an hour and a half away and I needed to be there this second.

Clearly I was in no position to drive, but I felt I would get back quicker if I did. Thankfully my keys were taken off off me and quite rightly so. I was aware that this was no time to be driving anywhere. My mum's partner came and took my car, following my mum and me back to my building site of a home.

That ninety minute journey felt like 10 hours, and I couldn't even tell you what was said, I have no idea.

I can't recall how I was told what had happened, everything was one big daze of shock. I was at Mum and Dad's, and my mum and her partner were back at my house waiting. No one really knew what they were waiting for other than for us girls to get home and to be told what had happened. My sister also had hours in the car to endure. She had moved away for university and was now living with her boyfriend in Epsom. I waited for her to arrive back in Somerset wondering how any of us were ever going to cope.

Shock and denial had taken over. Adrenalin was gushing through my veins, a haze of desperation and a startled look had firmly fixed itself on my face, the feelings and sounds of crying and panic are the only memories I have of the next eight hours. Maybe we had a cup of tea at some point, perhaps even some sleep, but I very much doubt it. Clearly I had been told the details of how my adorable brother had taken his own life, in fact as I am re-living the moment right now as I write, I think I was told in their kitchen.

Mum and Dad standing up against the kitchen worktops, with me sat on the floor, I vaguely remember.

The pain of knowing my sister was still trying to make her way home with the same level of desperation was unbearable. My other sister had only just had her first child, the first grandchild of the family. How was she ever going to be able to cope with this?

How can there be a tomorrow? What are we all supposed to do now? It felt like we were going to remain in this kitchen and hide for the rest of our lives, just the four of us. How would it be possible to face anyone else ever again? Everything had changed. I couldn't go home, I couldn't leave Mum and Dad, I couldn't go back and continue working on my home (my building site).

I had no idea how we were all supposed to go to bed after such a day. So much emotion and more tears than you ever thought anyone could cry. The sheer exhaustion must have sent us all to bed for a few hours; you open your eyes desperate to discover that it was a nightmare but no, the nightmare was real life.

This couldn't be real, it's something that only happens to other people or in films, not us...

The storm was followed by silence, a dreadful, painful silence which felt like a force in its own right. A line of questioning that seemed to go on for hours and hours followed. No one had ever imagined they would be asking such questions, but with no idea in the world that something like this could happen, it's amazing what gaps needed to be filled. There were no signs of depression, there were no drugs or alcohol involved, Callan didn't even smoke. He was just about to take his G.C.S.Es and was a *straight A* student with his whole life ahead of him, which had only ever seemed full of prospects.

NO NOTE? NO EXPLANATION? Then how do all our questions get answered? Why didn't you want us to know your reasons? So many questions and barely any answers, how was it possible to gain any understanding, and why did we even need any understanding to make anything clearer to us, when nothing was going to change the facts; nothing was going to bring my brother back.

My sister came home with me. It seemed like the right decision to make. Mum and Dad should be on their own and have some time to talk or just cry, or do whatever it is you do when you have just lost your son. We were scared about leaving them but it was important that they didn't have to deal with our grief as well as their own at this time. We held each other all night and didn't get much sleep but somehow managed to get about an hour after our incapacitated bodies decided to give up for the night.

The incomprehensible arrangements that my parents would now need to start, was a constant reminder of our reality. How is anyone in a position to decide what the funeral is to be like when they can't even believe that their loved one has even gone? It was all too much.

My next steps were to cancel life for a while, that was one thing I was certain of. There was no way I was going to work on Monday, how could I even think about work or even telling them at work why I was unable to come in? There was also no way the builder could come around as arranged. In order to cancel life, I had to continue doing. What an irony; *how do people actually just cancel life for a while, if you disappear, everything still goes on around you and could actually cause you more stress than if you just face a few things and cancel life properly. Was that even possible?*

Calling work and cancelling builders didn't seem to have any importance anymore and took more energy than I had. I was already well into any reserves of energy but told myself that after these few phone calls, that would be it. By calling, I had not burnt any bridges for the future and would not find myself in any awkward situations. I had given myself permission to log-out for a bit to deal with what was in front of me and these were the drivers that pushed me to get it together and make the necessary calls.

Maybe I would want to have a cup of tea, but that meant going to the shops to get milk. Once I had done that, then I was most definitely cancelling life. I soon realised that for everyone else, life just continued. People buzzing around the shops and talking on their phones, multi-tasking with their kids and talking to me as if nothing had happened. Of course they were, how were they to know what I was going through? I wasn't ready for this, I just wanted milk for a cup of tea, and to sit down and cancel life. No normality, no visits again to any shop, and certainly no conversations with anyone until I had figured out how to talk to anyone without blurting out what has just happened to me and what a state I am in.

I didn't know what to do other than get home and close the door behind me as quickly as possible.

That weekend, I made phone calls to friends and sent messages about what had happened to ease my guilt for ignoring every phone call I received. I wanted the world to know so that everyone would just stop with me for a day. It seemed rude all these strangers just carrying on without a care in the world, but at the same time, I didn't want to tell a soul, I couldn't explain it to myself let alone to anyone else.

Soon, work protocol had to be followed, so a meeting was arranged with management to discuss what was going to happen with my customer accounts and the business emails. There really was no shutting off from this world; I couldn't seem to find a way. The time I did have to myself just drove me mad with the same questions running through my head and no fixed answers, just a wild imagination that could conjure up any answer that I felt like giving myself in that moment.

Maybe it was best to just go back to work. My sister had returned now to her partner, my other sister had enough to focus on with her baby boy, and Mum and Dad had to deal with more than anyone should have to take in life, so where did that leave me? On my own in a house that was desperate for some tender love and care, with a job that needed to be maintained in order to pay my new mortgage and bills every month, and without a loving arm to hold me every night.

Now this really felt like the end. Had I reached the end of this journey already? Just when I thought I had gone through all the bad I could in life, I knew in this moment that I had to think about my future and whether it was going to be possible later on down the line to continue as I was. Would I ever be happy again? I didn't know the answers to those questions right now, which seemed better than a definite *no*. There was no place for arbitrary decisions right now, as I was fully aware that how I acted now could change the path of my future. Understanding this meant I was able to make the decision not to make any decisions right now. As my dad quoted throughout my teenage years 'In the face of all evil, all good men need to do, is nothing.' Similar wording from the original Edmund Burke quote 'The only thing necessary for the triumph of all evil is to do nothing.' This seemed to fit right now. Do nothing, I told myself, but be available to tell people that I am doing nothing. That way, no bridges are burnt when I do decide to do something. That included telling the man I had been speaking closely with for a little while now, that I was no longer able to communicate due to tragic circumstances. I had no idea what or who I needed so it was best to be alone until I had a few things figured out.

So many times, I have seen people chopping and changing their minds with the decisions they make, and justifying each rash decision during times when stillness seems to be the only decision one should make. Certainly it's a case of each to their own in times like these, but surely when you don't have the answers or you are fuelled by emotion, it is best to be patient. As we know, patience is not something that I usually possess but that's only when I have a clear understanding of the path I am taking. At this time of my life, everything was unclear and there was no telling when it would become clear.

Was this uncertainty that surrounded me going to ruin my life though? Would it hold me back for ever more? Not knowing the answers to those questions was enough to make me realise that the only way to escape this uncertainty was yet again, to take control of the situation and make some solid decisions soon.

That was enough for now, the fact that I had decided that this would need addressing was enough to tire me out. I fell back into my haze.

The family pulled in tightly and we were never too far from one another. We needed each other more than ever and we were all there in every way possible. It was the true test of a family, especially a split family: *If only Callan could see us now; he would have been so proud*.

Two weeks had passed and I was in my management meeting telling them how I needed to get back to work. Here we go again I thought, trying to convince other people to listen and trust in me and my decisions, but this time it wasn't working, and I was sent home for another two weeks to have some rest. They didn't realise that I didn't want to rest, I didn't want to be on my own all day and all night for the next two weeks, I wanted to be out of the house and focusing again—I didn't want to go mad.

They had made the right decision and they knew it. I must have looked exhausted, even though I put on my best suit and washed my hair, there was no hiding the pain on my face.

117

I couldn't have held a conversation with any customers anyway about their mundane rubbish (quite literally as I worked in the waste industry as a sales executive).

Rest is what I got; lots of walks on my own and rest. I decided I would respond to my friend again. I explained that I was unsure of what I was doing or what I wanted but just talking was nice. Some days I felt like it and others I didn't. Talking to anyone who had not experienced the things in life that I had, made it difficult for anyone to relate to me, no matter how hard they tried, and this caused a build-up of frustration within me. You know what it's like when you are talking to someone and they say they understand, you instantly think "no you don't, how could you possibly?" even though you appreciate their sympathy. Others say, "I couldn't imagine what you are going through right now", and all you can feel is agreement with them, making you feel as though there is a wall between you. What can be said to someone who has experienced such traumatic times? Just being there and being a good listener is worth more than anything, and this is what I had found in my new friend; someone who didn't claim to understand or show how many miles apart we are, but someone who was there and allowed me to reach out, as and when I felt comfortable; he allowed me to just be me.

As cold as it sounds, and as cold as it felt at the time, I had to do something that meant I wasn't giving up, so sitting around the house thinking was not getting me anywhere. It was another simple decision that just had to be made. Nothing was going to change what had happened, and nothing was going to help me right now, but by understanding that, I hoped that I could still function and carry on with at least the minimum required to keep life ticking by without any added stress, like mortgage payment issues or losing my job that I was doing so well in.

However irrelevant on the grand scale of things those minor issues may seem, they were creating the life I wanted. With only one life on this planet, I aim to make it as enjoyable as possible. I had to alter my thought process again to match this theory, as you can't feel so strongly about something like that and not apply it to all circumstances. *One day, we will all be gone and this will be a tale that is not even told. How many thousands of people die around the world every minute we take a breath?*

The world doesn't stop spinning each time for them; I don't get to hear about it, so why should this be any different? I muttered to myself. It is whatever we want it to be, just like everything else in life. It doesn't mean that the pain or grief is any less, and it doesn't mean that you don't ache in the same way as the next person, but it does mean you have a better chance of happiness again, and easing those terrible feelings.

Grief is a very consuming emotion. I read that it can take 18-24 months before you start feeling it ease (It takes as long as it takes). I know that grief affects people in different ways, sometimes a loss is not always sad, but there may be some regrets. Sometimes it's the worst thing that could ever happen to you, and the emotions are uncontrollable, the loss can be too much to take and you can even feel a complete loss of identity. In all cases one thing that doesn't change is that you were born with the ability to feel and love, and that ability has developed over the years. It is a gift to us, but with it also comes sadness. You can't have the rainbow without the rain. The worst element of grief varies with each individual, which makes talking about it very difficult for many. It can separate you from the people you know, as it's one of the only times in life, that even the people closest to you, may not understand—even the people who are grieving with you are not experiencing what you are experiencing, so there is still room for misunderstanding.

Having come to terms with this, I figured it was best to not have any expectations of how others may be able to help me, and certainly not to worry about how I would be judged for anything I did. We are all different; we deal with things in the way we feel is best, but sometimes, you can stumble across some advice that fits well with your own mantra and work with it, and that's exactly what I did.

What I wanted

Knowing that I wasn't really going to be able to help any of my family other than listen when they wanted me to, or just be there for a cuddle or coffee when needed, I knew this now had to be about what I wanted. Lonely, but *maybe I could choose how I deal with this?*

I already knew that I wouldn't end up hosting a self-pity party for long, as that's not my style, but the endless analysis and state of confusion on top of the heart wrenching emotions were enough to send me into a very dark state. I couldn't spend the rest of my days like that. *How would I have a family of my own, if I continue this dark state?* Oh no, that question led to more dark places. Do I even want to risk having a family of my own now, if this is the sort of thing that can happen? These questions and feelings are the effects of bad experiences, and they need to be addressed. They don't just go away by trying to ignore them, and if left un-addressed, they may even pop up again in later life as an issue, so I needed to address them immediately.

By interrogating myself further to find out the real truth of what I wanted at that time, I was able to make sure I understood why I would have such thoughts (the why), which in my case was fear of loss again, or fear of not being able to protect. Then I could reply to myself with the reality (the answer). In my case the reality was, that these things happen in life but you cannot try to avoid LIFE due to fear. Look at all the wonderful people that have happy families, look at yourself, you have managed to pull through hard times and still be there for your parents; this tragedy is not the 'norm'. Everybody has fears and you know that you must see the reality and not let those fears take over your reality. Telling myself this, really helped.

I love that feeling when you really understand yourself; when you know what you have to do, or know what you really want—or better still, what you don't want.

You can only work with facts, and they won't change. So what can I change?

I only want life with that person in it, who has now gone, so everything else is irrelevant. Is that irrelevant, considering it is still your one life that you have been given on this earth? Was there a life for you before that person, and regardless of how much you loved him and how hurt you are now, could there be a life without him?

If there could be a life without him, then why make it a miserable one? Does it just make you feel closer to him when you are suffering? Is it possible to feel just as close when you are happy and full of his memories in a positive way?

Who makes the right and wrong on this other than you?

Do I have to move on or can I just call it a change of direction? I don't like the term needing to move on, I don't agree with having to move on as it makes me feel like I have to forget that person; I don't want to forget or even move on, I want to pick myself up, find a direction again and bring you along with me in my heart. I won't feel guilty for wanting to pick myself up because you chose to take your life, but I didn't give you permission to take mine. You changed my life, but while I'm here, I'm going to carry on with my plan no matter how much I miss you.

These were many of my thoughts, which I don't mind sharing with you. They make sense to me, and perhaps to you, but as we are all individuals, and as our circumstances are all unique, gaining a true perspective of the way someone deals with something can be very difficult. All this information helps when choosing to model yourself on someone in order to try and gain the same achievements.

In my practice as an NLP therapist, I sometimes use the modelling technique, which is used widely in NLP; it looks at someone you aspire to be like. You would look at what that person has achieved, and how they have achieved it, and try to follow the same path. You would match their attitude and follow their steps in order to achieve the same, or at least something similar, and you would even go as far as understanding their thought processes.

This is quite tricky when most people don't divulge their thought processes, and even if they do, they only usually share with you the parts they want you to know. So that is another reason of mine for including my thought processes in this book. Some people question whether this means you are really being you if you are modelling yourself on someone else but the answer to that is simply that as long as you are true to yourself and what you want, then the answer is yes.

If we have the ability to be versatile and try new things, then there is no difference when trying a new way of thinking. As long as it fits with your core values, environment, capabilities, spirituality or purpose, behaviour, and your self-belief system, then there is no reason why you should not model yourself on someone who has achieved all that you, too, want to achieve (in NLP these six areas of your life are called the neurological levels).

All my answers came to me as time went on and my path barely changed. Of course I still want children; I always have done, so why should that change?

There are uncertainties in all areas of life, and if we are going to be ruled by fear or negativity, then we may as well resign ourselves now to a miserable existence. I would rather take the risks in life for a shot at some more happiness than never risk anything. It seemed that my mind was made up, I wanted direction again and I didn't want it to be a struggle.

We may not be able to control the things that happen in life but we can control our rationale.

Eight large drops of water just landed on this page while writing, smudging the ink. Water coming from my nose? Must be a release! I'll put that down to the emotions I feel when writing this on paper.

The suit was back on. At work I started on some light duties that were non-customer based. I still wasn't ready to hear people whinging about their cardboard collection, and I wasn't even sure that I would have the control to refrain from shouting obscenities at them if they even tried it. It was definitely wise to stick me behind a computer for now.

I appreciated being back in work though, surrounding myself with people was tricky, but the focus and itinerary was something that I was thankful for; they eased me back into a life where I would have to start thinking about other things again.

Are you your friend?

Driving back from work today, I decided to pick up my pen and paper again this evening. It's been about a month and a half now since I've even looked at this pad (that's apart from the rough sketch I did on the back page where I had started designing the new bathroom). Now I'm typing the book up, the bathroom is nearly finished (the joys of a whirlpool bath and a powerful shower). It's the last room in the house to be renovated, and will complete the task I started just over two years ago. I'm finally seeing the fruits of my labour. It was this moment that I had been working towards when making all those decisions about returning work and the way I approached certain things. I even changed jobs just over a year ago to something much better paid in order to speed up the process.

Now that I am there, I am able to enjoy the relaxing evenings I visualised. I feel very lucky, although being realistic, none of it has been down to luck, but hard graft and careful planning.

I had planned to make a start on this book but had to wait for the creativity to flow. There are some things in life you can plan and as we all know, other things just happen or have to be put off due to prioritising. Sometimes, I want to do everything at once and the ideas take over my mind, but I find, rather than getting bogged down with it all and procrastinating, I make lists, set goals and priorities.

When prioritising, you should bear in mind all aspects of your life. I knew this book would bring me some peace and happiness as well as keeping me focused on doing the things I enjoy and hopefully helping others along the way. There's no backing out now, no matter how many negative thoughts I may have or how much fear of the unknown I may feel. That's the ridiculous thing about fear, it often involves something unknown. There were various questions in my mind that mainly focused on the negatives, I can see why it would put a lot of people off doing the things they want to do, but here's the thing: it doesn't have to.

If you want something badly enough, you will find a way of getting it and once you know how to prevent negative thoughts from taking over, then you allow yourself the opportunities in life to do whatever you want to.

I share my thoughts with you throughout this book so that you can analyse them and even compare them to your own. When watching other people succeed, even in the face of adversity, it's simple to see how they have done it when you have the full picture. As mentioned earlier about watching people on stage and listening to their stories of triumph but not actually really knowing how they managed to get there. Everything came down to their thoughts and then the committed decisions they made.

Who would read this book anyway? I am not sure that anyone would want to read about all my woes and reasoning. This was one of the first thoughts that came to mind after I had come to the decision to start my writing journey. Initially I was just full of enthusiasm and excitement at the prospect of getting my story out there, but when I actually made a start, this was the first of a string of thoughts that could have quite easily stopped me in my tracks. The only reason it didn't, was because I understand my mind and the power of reasoning.

The ability to then delve further into these thoughts and make sure that what you are thinking is actually realistic, is where the art of positive thinking starts. *I don't actually know if anyone would read my book, but that doesn't really matter, as long as I do what I am setting out to do and get enjoyment from it. In this world we have to just give it a shot so that is what I am going to do. Who knows, it might even get published straight away and become the next big thing.* Now that was more like it, a great answer to a negative question. All I do is look for the better outcome and focus on it, which becomes the driver. This positive thought process wasn't there at the start, I had to unravel my true *want* and play devil's advocate with myself. For some, this can take days, weeks, even years. On this occasion it took me about two minutes, but it is this process that helps many of the people I speak to. Rather than stop yourself at the first moment of negativity, then let it take over and form a mist over your options, it's better to understand it and hold an argument with yourself until the answers you really need in order to succeed are there.

Me a writer? You don't read enough books for that. You don't have a good enough vocabulary to be a writer. Most writers have been to university and read the newspaper every day. What a ridiculous thought, that would do nothing positive for me at all. The rationale here was simple: *I don't expect it to be everyone's cup of tea, but it doesn't have to be (they are the lyrics of another great song I have been recently listening to). Of course, there are critics in everything we do but that doesn't need to affect me. I mustn't be scared of other people damaging what I love, we all have an opinion and mine is just as valid as the next person's. I am humble and not trying to make out that I know it all, I just know that the people I have helped and the process I use works for them as well as for me, so why not write about it? I don't agree with everything that I have read before now, and there's nothing wrong with that. I could even cover that in my book, to make me feel better and give me the extra confidence I need to make this happen. That is exactly what the book is about right? Anyway, exactly how many books do you need to read before being qualified to write one yourself?* It seems the rationale had worked. I was back on track and excited again. Now when typing this up, it makes so much sense to me. I even wanted to delete that last thought because since writing it, I have only had positive thoughts while

131

enjoying the flow of the book, but I think it's important to retain everything, on the off-chance it may help you.

No matter how I reasoned with myself about writing this book, I still noted that it was an awful thing to tell myself. Telling myself that I couldn't be a writer because I hadn't been to university or because I don't read a newspaper every day is ridiculous. What a stereotypical definition, and how limiting for myself. It got me thinking about the way that we talk to ourselves, and how everyone should be aware, and tune in to what is being said. You wouldn't talk to a friend like that, you would encourage them to follow their dreams and passions; you would support them and help them where possible; so why do so many of us struggle to give ourselves the same level of support? In most things you do, you will probably find there doesn't need to be a conscious level of reasoning as we are fully capable of doing things through habit, and are quick to understand our *'why'*, but jumping out of your comfort zone usually requires effort.

You are writing a book on positivity and here you are telling yourself all the reasons why it couldn't work! The difference is, I am telling myself these things in a way of exploration in order to push myself through any objections. I am used to doing this now, and confident that I will act in a way that will push myself forward in the desired direction. I just need to make sure that the direction is one that I want.

That comes with evaluating all eventualities, including criticism in this case. It's no problem having these thoughts, just as long as you find a better way of thinking about it so that you are not swayed only by negativity.

Here I am nearly half way through my writing journey, still finding out the differences between people who really want something and the people who are just dabbling with ideas which I see all the time. Nothing really comes of it unless there is a true underlying persistence and passion for a particular outcome. I look at things from all angles, giving myself an opportunity to back out should it be something that I don't really want to do. It's the power of having a goal that you truly want, which gives you the capability to think positively.

Look out for your own best interests because no one else in life will have the same level of commitment to making the things that you want most to happen, other than you.

It is clear that the successful people I have spoken with over the years are the people that have cared for themselves. They are the people who have taken responsibility for their own path and owned their journey. Being kind to yourself and allowing yourself to explore all possibilities can only enhance your life. Those around you that are important should only support you in that journey and help you when needed.

Being that friend to myself, is what saved me from the terrifying and bleak road that was being offered as an alternative path. The friend in me asked the right questions and wasn't scared about finding out the honest answers.

The next big question that followed when I was caught up in grief was, 'what's important to me now?'

Nothing seemed as important to me anymore, and everything needed to be re-evaluated. The renovation at that time no longer had the same importance—what was the point? I didn't feel that I could simply carry on as normal. It was all very well going back to work on light duties and earning my money so that my bills were paid, but actually starting up again doing the things that were so important to me, seemed impossible.

Over the next month, I realised that I would find more peace if I was in an organised and cosy home. Walking across floorboards with nails in them and looking around at patches of unfinished plastering wasn't actually helping me heal. There was another reason to get this project started again. It wasn't because I didn't care and life had to go on, but it was the next step I needed to make to be able to feel peace. Before long, the builders were back in and the house renovation had begun again; this time for different reasons and with a different feeling, but it had started again nonetheless.

The answer to my question about what was now important to me was my family; my family was the most important thing in my life but I was already doing everything I was capable of to show that.

The next important thing to me was my own peace, and the ability to heal, followed by the importance of trying to prevent this from happening to anyone else. Although an impossible task, I asked myself again if there was anything I could do that would at least bring awareness and help. The answers flashed through my mind, I could raise money for charity which would cover these three most important things in my life—my family, myself and others who may be susceptible to such pain. This was sure to be a good start, amongst the medley of grief, confusion and borderline apathy, there lay all my answers.

Peru

The fundraising had started for my trip to Peru. Oh! I've decided to go to Peru have I? No turning back now, people have already started to donate. I had decided to trek the Inca Trail to raise money for Mind, the mental health charity. Funnily enough, we stumbled across a bucket list when clearing out my brother's room and on the top of that bucket list was The Inca Trail in Peru. I have travelled for many years and seen many wonders of the world but never had I done such a challenge.

I was to go on my own as I didn't want to have to talk to anyone, I would use that time for peace and healing for myself and in the process, it would help my family to focus on something positive and as a result, help other people through the charity who may be suffering or at risk. It was the perfect solution that fitted all my priorities in life.

I'd better start training then! I think I had only been to the gym a handful of times in my life so I didn't underestimate the training that would be involved in trekking eight hours a day for four days at an altitude of 4,300 meters. Dead woman's pass was the part of the itinerary that scared me the most, and I questioned whether I would be fit enough to complete it. There was no time at all for any doubting of myself here as all my energy needed to be channelled into making it possible, and that meant researching and getting as fit as I needed to be in order to complete this challenge. There was always more to it than just setting myself a challenge to earn money for charity, it seemed that I had found the ideal solution, which meant that I would have to get out the house and put myself into new surroundings when training for an entire year. This meant hiking mountains at the weekends and going off in all types of weather, being close to nature and the great outdoors, which played a huge part in my healing. I enjoyed it!

The raising money part helped me to meet new people and talk about my story. It showed me a world of people who were just wonderful and caring, it showed me how many people that we pass most days have gone through very similar tragedies. It opened up a whole new world for me and I felt like I was doing the right thing.

I realised that my goal of just getting back to normality was a little bit small minded and that I could set my goals even higher if I wanted to. I could create change for others, not just myself; I could grow as a person more than I had ever believed; I could have an even better life than I had before the loss of my brother; and all without any guilt. I allowed myself to feel excited again. It was ok because my brother was my inspiration, and you can't feel any closer to someone than that. No longer did the tears and sadness bring me closer to my brother, but each step I took that brought a positive change in my life made me feel closer to him. Each person that I helped, and each pound that was raised for my chosen charity, made me feel like he was next to me.

The other options now looked even more depressing than before. I still get upset and sad now, and in every four or five hour period I will think of him in some way (unless I'm sleeping, but sometimes, he's even there in my dreams or nightmares). I'm comfortable with that, he's in my heart and he still feels constant. Last year there wasn't a 30 minute slot when my brother wasn't on my mind in some way.

After months of training, leaving the house early to set out on my blustery 26 mile walks with a backpack full of weights and running uphill on the treadmill at the gym, I was ready for my trek. Having raised £3,450.00 for my chosen charity, a lot of people were following me.

I decided to trek the Inca Trail without my prosthetic lens. This would have been the first time in 10 years that I would meet new people without wearing my lens, which was a very unsettling thought. I was pushing myself completely out of my comfort zone, but for more reasons than to just give it a go. I had realised that it wouldn't be the most sterile of trips and that any possibility of an eye infection had to be avoided.

There was another plus point to not wearing my lens, here was a great opportunity to meet people with their own reasons for embarking on such an adventure, who may be more understanding than the general public. It also seemed like the perfect opportunity to conquer any fears in my life that I may have been carrying.

I had become dependent on my lens, but I didn't see that as a problem as it would always be there with me as an option.

I knew deep down, that I would be able to get out there without it if I really had to, but I also knew it would benefit me to leave without it. I hoped that if nothing else, it would help others who followed me realise that we all have issues and fears that can be overcome, if we just put our minds to it. Sometimes to others, it looks like I just plough through life with great ease, overcoming any challenge or hurdle that's thrown my way. I may come across as someone for whom everything is very balanced and clear, so it's a great opportunity for me to let you know how it's been done, what my thoughts are and to show you the fears I have faced.

Arriving at the airport and meeting the first five people who were also trekking made me quite nervous. I am usually an outgoing and confident person, and situations like this would never phase me, but without my false eye, I felt like someone else. They looked at me differently to what I had become used to (not that they would have been any the wiser). There didn't seem to be any element of judgement, but the human brain can't help but wonder what has happened to someone when you see a physical defect. I used another rationale: *I don't have to explain and no one needs to know, they are meeting me for the first time and will get to know me for who I am as a person if they choose, and not based on what I look like. This is perfect!*

The trek was awesome. So much beauty everywhere — beauty in the people I trekked with, and beauty in the outstanding nature that surrounded me. It was my heaven on earth.

My training had paid off, I completed the trek and stayed ahead all the way, there was no waiting for me. I had a soul full of determination and a passion for what I was doing, which was for so many people, including my brother. It had been a long journey to get to this point and

I felt the biggest relief when I was there. No social media or phones, just me, myself and I.

I think I made it sound easy on my return; it wasn't, in fact, there were a few tears and a few moments when I questioned whether I was able to go any further, but I kept pushing on and reached that highest point I was working towards, 'Dead Woman's Pass' (I completely understand why it was called this now). What a relief, as I reached that point, a picture was taken and I knew the hardest part was over. Donations were still coming in when I was out there, the support was immense and that kept me going. Part of me didn't want it to end, and then there was the other part of me that was desperate for a rest and a bath. My feet needed some attention, and I craved a comfortable bed after sleeping in a shared tent at camp every night. Ten days away from home in total with travelling time was enough for me; I was desperate to see my family, who had been following my progress as well as they could via GPS.

Arriving back home was emotional. There was a huge sense of achievement, but at the same time, it was all over now. Everything I had focused on for the last 12 months had now reached an end and I wondered whether this would take some adjusting to.

The process

I've met some very positive people along my way but there's more to it than just a few clichés and great quotes. This is why I wanted there to be a process to look at when writing this book, and it's simple: BFA

- ❖ Be a friend to yourself
- ❖ Find alternative/better solutions (for your negative circumstances and thoughts)
- ❖ Action the small steps first (keeping your goal/goals in mind)

By putting these things in to practice and actually making changes, you naturally pick up a more positive outlook. As the pace of breaking through barriers increases, your self-belief grows.

Never stop questioning, as life changes continuously, and the more understanding of yourself you have, the quicker your answers will come.

Eventually the negative thoughts that initiate the questioning may even stop all together, making daily living a lot more peaceful. The quicker your answers come, the more decisions you can make, and the easier and more fulfilling life becomes.

I recently read the quote 'we are not trees, we don't have to stay put to grow'. I love this phrase because unless we are truly happy with every aspect of our life, and we do not strive for anything more, then we must continue to move. Sometimes, that may just mean moving with the times.

Positive people understand themselves and what they want. They may not know how to get there exactly but they have a great outlook which will help them. It doesn't mean that they always get it right or that life doesn't sometimes get them down, but it does mean that they search for more answers and give themselves a better chance of happiness than someone who is stuck in a negative loop. Choose wisely as that's all it is, a choice that is the result of one single question.

Where to start

It's easier to train yourself to become more positive than many people think. Of course, when enduring hard times, the pain doesn't just vanish, the headache of knowing which way to turn still remains, but you find your solution more quickly, and you can virtually guarantee that a solution will be found.

Knowing your own thought processes is a great place to start, tune in completely and listen to how you talk to yourself, that along with practising good questioning means you are starting to *action for change.*

I spoke earlier about that *chitter chatter* that we all have going on inside our heads; some coaches and therapists, including myself, refer to this *chitter chatter* as NATS (Negative Automatic Thoughts).

As most of us have NATS, regardless of how we deal with them, a great place to start is by tuning in to them and actually highlighting them.

You can do this by forming a simple chart on paper, or even a spreadsheet; something simple like the one on the next page is often used in my therapy sessions.

You might be surprised about the type of things you say when you start listening to yourself.

Negative Thought	Situation	Reality of thought %	Balancing statement
He thinks I'm fat	He walked out the house without saying this dress looks good on me	I know he always compliments me and he was rushing to get to work – he may not have noticed the dress but has never called me fat. Perhaps I'm the one that doesn't feel too good in it. 5%	He is rushing to get to work. I'll show him my dress later when he gets home. I think he will like it.

Negative Thought	Situation	Reality of thought %	Balancing statement
No one likes me in this office	Walked in to work this morning and no one said hello	How often do they say hello to me? Not often but some do smile at me. Maybe they don't say it all the time because I don't say it either. It doesn't necessarily mean that they dislike me. 20%	I'll say good morning to everyone tomorrow and see if they say hello or morning back. I am sure they will. It will be nice to speak to everyone for a change.

In my example, you will see that by being honest with yourself and not getting carried away with one recurring negative thought process, you are able to determine how true your negative thought really is. I have given a percentage in my example. Usually anything under 50% is very unlikely to be true, and anything over 50% may need some more attention.

By writing down a *balancing thought,* which is just an alternative, better thought, that could also fit your situation, you are exploring some other options. It is best if this balancing thought also includes an action which may help you to make an improvement.

So you will see in the first example, the action is to go into work and be the first person to say hello in the morning. This will give a more accurate reality of the negative thought.

It's difficult to see the reality for what it is sometimes when we get carried away with our thoughts, usually because our own story gets in the way.

This technique has been used by many people who have turned their thoughts around to seek a better result in their life, and it actually works.

Have a go yourself on the next page.

Use this book to keep a log and refer back to if necessary.

Negative Thought	Situation	Reality of thought %	Balancing statement

Team6 Motivation

During my time training for the Inca Trail, I decided that it would also be a good time to start that business venture. I had already been building it up and creating a following beforehand, but it seemed like a good time to take a serious plunge at giving it a good shot, and that meant making some committed decisions.

The name Team6 was inspired by my parents, a long time before we lost Callan. A car had arrived at my dad's work place with a number plate on it that said TEAM6. Dad said that this was going to be a family number plate for when we all go into business together. As there were six of us, it seemed fitting. We had often talked about running a family business, like a guest house by the sea, but with so many personalities in our family, finding something that we would all want to do was difficult. Not much more thought ever really went into it.

When Callan died, we lost our number 6. Our team had been broken. This hurt all of us and the thought of Team6 not ever amounting to anything upset me whenever I thought of my long-term business plans.

It hadn't all been erased from my mind though, there was no reason I couldn't set my business up and use the name Team6, as our little number '6' hadn't gone in my mind but had now become a force (something like a spiritual force that was pushing me forward and inspiring me to do more).

That was the birth of Team6 Motivation. The website was being built and the videos had started. My trek was announced and I was followed through personal and social media channels, as well as online through my business. Radio interviews, newspaper articles and blogs helped me to develop the business further. Upon my return from Peru I visited schools, where I would stand up in front of the pupils and deliver my talks. So when I arrived back home and wondered whether I was going to feel a void, or manage to adjust again after having spent the last 12 months focusing on the Inca Trail, it was apparent that my journey had only really just begun.

I wanted to turn everything around, and that is what I continue to do each day—work towards achieving the things I want and having more time to do the things I love, as well as grow and improve as a person along the way.

Writing this book has helped me in my quest to do so, just as much as the other aspects of my business (although I am still waiting for my dad's number plate).

Team6 Motivation has many branches, allowing me to head off in any direction suits me at a particular time, and put all my skills into use. I enjoy a variety of things in life, and this was one of the key goals for me when deciding what to do; *find something that gives you the freedom to choose what to focus on according to your mood. Give yourself a number of areas in which you can grow in. Give yourself that variety in life that you love* I told myself – that's exactly what I did. From sales and customer service training (putting my years of sales success to good use) to speaking at events, running workshops, coaching, mentoring and writing in between. I had all of my business passions catered for. I allocated time to becoming a practitioner, therapist and coach, which all seemed a bit far-fetched when I first started out, but with the same philosophies, I applied myself as and when I could, taking the first small steps that were needed to gain the experience and certificates I required. Who would have thought after such trauma, I would be sitting here today writing about this journey? – I did! I thought it! I believed in it, and here you are by my side, investing your time in me as I invest my time in you. Team6 workshops keep me busy, along with Team6 talks where I get to enjoy networking and presentations from businesses. We are all here to learn as much as we can to improve our journey. What fits for some might not fit for others, but along the way, if we take just one useful tip or piece of advice from the information we gather, then it was worth investing that time.

No longer question 'if' you could do something but question 'how' you can do something, and find your starting point.

If you want to make good use of your time, you've got to know what's most important and then give it all you've got – Lee Lacocca

ABOUT THE AUTHOR

Louise H McClintock grew up with high hopes in a small Somerset town. After a rocky childhood where she witnessed tragedy and heartache from an early age, she developed an analytical mind that led her on a path of personal development.

Throughout her adult years there were to be many more mountains to climb before gaining a greater understanding of how to get the things in life you desire the most. Now as an NLP therapist, a CBT practitioner, life/business coach and motivational speaker, Louise has found her path to happiness.

As the founder of Team6 Motivation she is on a mission to help others along her way, telling her stories of tough times which made her only more determined to bring about change.

Meet Callan's monkey that travelled the Inca Trail with me.

A very photogenic monkey who was the best company I could have hoped for. Monkey does love a good holiday and the odd beer.

He is looking forward to the next challenge in the Sahara Desert.

Until next time – I bid you farewell.

#Team6motivation

Made in the USA
Middletown, DE
10 September 2017